Advanced Praise for *Here*

Colin Browne's panoramic scenes balance finely in humble and learned detail. Cinematic syntax, built frame-by-frame, slide-by-slide in a textured carousel. Fragments of history, memory, literary instances dart across the globe perceiving and questioning through transitions and improvising pivots – where *would be the self opening the door to the inhuman*, where *it was a long way to go to right a wrong*, where *stolen land is a cash machine*, where *what seeps up from the earth's heart*, where *those who witnessed nothing*, where *a hunter enters with his skinning knife to discover himself within* – to land us *Here*. A lockdown traveller's wing, *Here* is a time-machine in a pocketbook.

—**Laiwan**, author of *TENDER*

In *Here*, Browne writes portraits of place, weaving artefacts and animals, thinkers and artists. Birds glide between text connecting people, loss, languages, histories, and landscapes to magnify experiences of impermanence, presence, and emplacement.

—**Leanne Dunic**, author of *One and Half of You*

I0809495

Also by Colin Browne

POETRY

Abraham
*Ground Water**
*The Hatch**
*The Properties**
*The Shovel**

PROSE

*Entering Time: The Fungus Man Platters of Charles Edenshaw**
I Had an Interesting French Artist to See Me This Summer: Emily Carr and Wolfgang Paalen in British Columbia
Motion Picture Production in British Columbia, 1898–1940: A Brief Historical Background and Catalogue

*Published by Talonbooks

Here

POEMS

Colin Browne

TALONBOOKS

Talonbooks
9259 Shaughnessy Street, Vancouver, British Columbia, Canada V6P 6R4
talonbooks.com

Talonbooks is located on xʷməθkʷəy̓əm, Sḵwx̱wú7mesh, and səl̓ilwətaʔɬ Lands.

First printing: 2020

Typeset in Minion
Printed and bound in Canada on 100% post-consumer recycled paper

Cover and interior design by Typesmith
Cover image: *Yachting in Vancouver Harbour* from the Vancouver Archives

Talonbooks acknowledges the financial support of the Canada Council for the Arts, the Government of Canada through the Canada Book Fund, and the Province of British Columbia through the British Columbia Arts Council and the Book Publishing Tax Credit.

Canada | Canada Council for the Arts | Conseil des arts du Canada | British Columbia | British Columbia Arts Council — An agency of the Province of British Columbia

Library and Archives Canada Cataloguing in Publication

Title: Here : poems / Colin Browne.
Names: Browne, Colin, 1946– author.
Identifiers: Canadiana 20200198386 | ISBN 9781772012644 (softcover)
Classification: LCC PS8553.R69 H47 2020 | DDC C811/.54—dc23

For my dear ones, and
especially for Sue, my sister

One day [Durus] returned in triumph from Batuan with a rare text he had discovered in the home of the *klian* in his village. It was a book of recipes and ingredients for the different feast dishes, written in verse [in Kawi, the old Javanese language]. But when I gave it to Madé Gria, the *dalang*, to read, he looked at it for some time, and at last, finding the stanzas unfamiliar, he said:

> I cannot read it, for I do not know the tune.
> But never mind the tune; just read the words.
> But he only repeated: I can't, I do not know the tune ...

—COLIN MCPHEE
A HOUSE IN BALI (1946)

For the story of Orpheus is of the truth.
For there was such a person a cunning player on the harp.
For he was a believer in the true God and assisted in the spirit.
For he playd upon the harp in the spirit by breathing upon the strings.
For this will affect every thing that is sustained by the spirit even
every thing in nature.
For it is the business of a man gifted in the word to prophecy good.

—CHRISTOPHER SMART
JUBILATE AGNO, XXIII (1759–1763)

When the films are finished it's
as if I'd made nothing but mist.

—CHANTAL AKERMAN
MA MÈRE RIT (2013)

folding and folding
upon itself
inner outer inner
one thing
boundless
turning, turning

es igual, said the *trabajadora de la noche*
to the jock
in Puerto Limón

Diorama

+

is it not unfolding as we imagined, are these not
the brass mackerels we welcomed home, is that
seven-headed god not the yellow box
we yelled for, is this not the street of the lost handshake
between Picasso and Breton, did the father not take
the mother to see the exhibition at war's end
is a wheelbarrow not the green room
bristling with forest spirits, is renunciation
not the new consumption, was there not
one lip-smacking lie that set the twentieth century
in motion, was the passerby not fatally
ambushed by desire, is the young man not
booking a flight to Turkey, are the barracks
not being aired out once again?

i lived in barracks, my father lived in barracks
my uncles lived in barracks, my grandfathers
lived in barracks, my great-grandfathers
lived in barracks, our Irish ancestor lived in barracks
to subdue *les Indiens*
and *les Canadiens*
in British North America
and was fed

grand fodder

+

Six and a quarter inches from the pitch of its head
to the blunt, square tip of its nose. You'd think
its eyes were burned in by almonds. On its crown
eight holes for the shafts of feathers. Without birds
the sky would be deaf. Holes drilled at the temples
to knot the gut, to make one face of two.
In the forehead, trapezoids, with plugs,
perhaps the eyes of its Person. Nostrils
so the Person can breathe. Teeth
precisely incised. The sweep that
narrows to its snout
holds my mind, the scoop
of eye sockets, cheeks rubbed red
with oil, their echo the orbit
the Person pursues, winding
beyond us within us.
How did it end up here, stripped
of its feathered crown?
That can be remedied, but don't we
need its intercession now,
aren't we overdue?

+

the year he travelled to the Mission at the river's mouth
in charge, he wrote, of the Unaligmiut
what was he thinking?

they had, by then, Russian names
and performed the Russian rites
in the old church on the island

the territorial wars were over
now the Unaligmiut are American
now he is in charge

now he intercedes
now they ask his permission
from here on in the U.S. Army will decide

should the U.S. Army dare to interfere
he's told, the Unaligmiut will leave
for the mountains and not return

said the Unalaklit Chief, *to stop the Eskimo*
singing and dancing would be like
cutting the tongue out of a bird.

+

in the rusted playground
tremors
hind legs so stiff
and the crow begins

on her eyes
she twists, jaw
snapping,
ducking, dodging

making herself small
in a hollow
below the swings
she circles

tucks her tail under
lifts her eyes
drops in
lets go

puts that old
head down

+

what did the great Popes do
& what happened to the multi-volume
sermon sets? bpNichol said
all you have to do is look, not read
and you will observe something rueful
you don't want homilies at any rate
no matter how cut about the mouth i've been
in the engine room of the SS *Homily*
i'd be glad to sit out the salt tablets
and sing ghazals
but back to those sermon sets
what were they thinking? from above
it looks like the first line of a novel –
a truck has rolled over
sewing machines spill out
into the snow beside a gash
in the earth left by what looks like
a single blow from the head
of a giant axe and the scene is crawling with
men in uniforms, did someone add that
"these people do not know that they are
separate from this mouth," i can't
remember, what did the great Popes declare
and was that source cleared, is anything
separate, or did i copy it down wrong?
severance, not separate, sore about the lips
in comes another barrage
the pickups speed toward Palmyra

with pocket money from connoisseurs
in Brunello Cucinelli knits
who'll mount a head of plundered curls
or a sledge-hammered
shank of the Bride
on a steel rod
in the hall
everyone knows
whose holds the oil's
pumped into
Julius II in 1512 decreed
that America's heathens
were descended from
Adam and Eve
he too was planning
to sell short

the poet and physician Yehuda ha-Levi of Cordova
held that language ascends through
hierarchies of perfection, warning
of wisdom "*that bears no fruit*
but only blossoms"
doesn't that sound terribly familiar?
on his pilgrimage to the Holy Land
it's said he received
a spear in the chest
from an Arab rider
beneath the walls
of Jerusalem
while singing
"Ode to Zion"

crag of cinders
hill of woe
your black smoke
is death nothing to you?
Noah in San Marco

buffeted dove
in a sea of vipers

i emerged in Atlantic light
a wee smoltie, aslant
a half step from a buttercup

i sang the baby in the basket
and the baby in the manger
if i should die before
i wake, i sang

i bound my liver
to the prophecies
until here was here
and set about
the exterminations

+

What, once gone
will find its way back?
And did you enjoy
your visit? So much
to see.
And the dioramas?
The artist spent years
under these lights
needle by needle
larch by larch
laying on ochre.
He lost the battle
for the clouds. But
it's too much, isn't it?
These chunky spear-
tossers beset by
silverfish and dry rot
in sodium gloom.
I can only take in
one gallery at
a time. Really, I'm
only here because
you're depressed.
The ibex or antelope
on the unfinished hills
seem overwrought.
Shouldn't they resemble
blobs? Jena was

a seabed heaving
with worms. What about
the women? Why
do they do that?
He's in the old quarter
now, working on
a new ocean
choked with bull-headed
flesh-ripping fish
dabbing glitter
on rollers.

Sing to me
of the beguiling
and the beguiled
the engines of
order and disorder
torn symmetries
and scrims
drowned towers
severed nations
delirium's blue
reflection
O lamb of
prosopopoeia
shaft of giant
fennel.

Witnesses spoke of
fury in the skies
over Galway
fairy legions battled
through the night
at dawn the fog cleared
then solid rain
and putrefaction
hurried pits

"old bones ...
among the rocks."
London sent
American corn
to dent the misery
Indian meal, it was
called, after those
it was stolen from

and the vessels
Naomi
Fanny
Agnes
Hannah
Maria
Marchioness of Abercorn
British Queen

A frigate from New Spain
put into Kichx̱áan
with sacks of the
sockeye's bridegroom.
We've been eating
them ever since
said the woman at
the family reunion.

Folding, enfolding
oneself into another
burr and rambler
runner and burr
I sow words
in this furrow
thinking to braid
love into the world.

Men and women
once flew to the moon
to beg for mercy
and may still.
The sky is a cloak
in winter
woven with
berries and bark.
Perhaps the first poem
was a prayer
the second a curse.
Orison's horizons.
Then the heartbroken
took to hammers.

Here's a device
with a throat
of singed lapis –
an oystercatcher
rattle. Its wings
and body are
beaten copper
lashed on with cord
its ivory beak
an amulet
is a sea-wolf
the man on its back
gazes at the moon
uncoupled from time
outward bound.
Oystercatcher
up to its knees
cocks its head.
What remains
of its song?
All of it.

Believing themselves
free men, my fathers
seized what they
could and hurled
their magic aside
that rending broke
my grandfather
into two men
or rather, one man
torn in two
with half a song.

He lies now
in a fairy mound
Gone west.
You may know
that he was buried
up to his chin
in France
and shipped home
in a dead man's skin.

What has become
of the songs
he sang?

Next week the artist
lays on primer
for the foreshore.
He'll pull a pippin
from his pocket
and a blade-cut
No. 2 Round.

Musical Chairs, or Travelling to Jerusalem – 1

For H.P.

wind's up
          i clap
serrations
clap
          /clasp
winds up
aspens
          /clap
clap

a man rips a pink blanket
from under a crumpled house

what a poet spies:
sometimes not much at all

west light bike light
stifled star
i had my six-pack on
my cetacean Tostitos
O mirth of my nation
glazed in stunt aspic, azure throated

insurrection bound
transactions in small bills only, please

the young cats are jamming with their Chet Baker hair
i'm getting kissed on the lips
it must be late
tree clams
out we
squirt

down the lane
a young guy with a gym bag
and a phone number
heads for the airport
Marian, your suitors are in the grove

a man digs out a green bicycle

who was that up on the bridge deck
beneath the cables
conversing with cloud-high Transparents?
was that you
riding the streetcar to the armoury in 1917
cracked chanter in your coat?
it's seen its tears
did i say stars
                    stags?
in her album, the English girl
wrote "*mowitch*"
packing one home on your shoulders
his legs hoofed braids
where did that happiness go?

two hundred white lorries
it's not what they are bringing in
it's what they are carrying home

my refuge is *p*, the kindest
mildest letter
a letter like a kerchief

sign on an industrial building
in Spandau
BLACKY DRESS

aspen, or elfin
mitten, or midden
calipers, or caliphate
Babel, or label

so far, or shofar
shofar, so far

he's in there with his trowel
sixty bucks a month
horny to boot
in the black earth
at midnight, prying
jawbones from clam shells
filling his sack

my tires unravel the upheaving street
a loader lifts a wall
me, me, cries the cursor
i'm molecules too

Bialik's sprites: *tzafririm*
"*Come enter my soul and shine!*"

the chairs are years

each day until last month
she listened beneath
the walnut tree
for the first morning bus on Main
"I'm still here,"
she'd say
"I'm *still* here."

Musical Chairs, or Travelling to Jerusalem – 2

> Palestine has produced nothing but religions, sacred frenzies, presumptuous attempts to conquer the outer world of appearances by the inner world of wishful thinking. And we hail from there.
>
> —SIGMUND FREUD to ARNOLD ZWEIG
> MAY 8, 1932, *LETTERS OF SIGMUND FREUD* (1961)

That outcrop where the old man knelt in confusion: did he trust that the
author of his misfortune, in an act of gallantry,

might reward his compliance on this bluff where kneeling men and
women, lives squirting out of them

were heaved onto the rocks below; where a stallion pushed off into the
stars, hooves sparking above the bonfires

where the boy, clutching kindling to his chest, ran ahead to console a
ram on a peak once swarmed by gods?

What adjective had run dry by the time Allenby seized the gate?

I can remember my father talking about one of their Sunday
afternoon sports, said Primrose Upton of Keremeos.

A man pulls a blanket out from under the smashed concrete, displays it
to the camera. Every day his street is pulverized from the air.

Some old Indian would go up the shale slide and throw
rattlesnakes out.

They need plasma, anaesthetics, bottled water in the basement surgery.
Dust stuccos lungs.

Various people would be put in various places down the shale slide,
and they'd whang these snakes on [the head] with sticks.

And now so-and-so and so-and-so refuse to travel abroad because of
particulates in the air, but when they really need to get away

a pal who's made a fortune profiteering from chronic medical conditions
associated with industrial and environmental degradation

will fly them over in his private jet.

And there'd be a count at the end of the afternoon. This was quite
an afternoon's fun for them.

What of the rattles? And was there a place laid at the table for that
"old Indian"?

Gallant. The word is *gallant.*

The Azure Notebook

+

I fear to cut the pearl from the bivalve.

—OSIP MANDELSTAM
"ARIOSTO" (1933)

four men around a table
listen for the killing
of engines – branches
arrested by rocks
mid-current –
one is sent to his
children in the beech wood
after collapsing

in September
the trucks return
now the forest is silent
snow lies undisturbed
who can say *hillside*
or *table* as if these words
offer refuge
or fraternity
as if they do not
tear the heart
in two?

Max Beckmann
your four
what of them?
i'm a son of bird-snarers
pit-lampers, poachers
scavengers, fixers
agents of desertification
we killed and killed again
our god deranged generations
i'm pliable, reliable
loyal to my clan
a monkey's fist
on a heaving line
to a hawser of grief

deception, duplicity
treachery, stealth
burrs sown
into my skull

+

a table is no ordinary thing
how can it be?
nothing is
not the limb, the lathe
the hands that held the saw
planks planed
stacked, cured
bolted and waxed
on the edge
one is not alone

sky mackerel
seed tosser
hillside drinker
in hard frost
sleet & flood
lake ascending
into clouds
pillar of spent fish
nation of deliverance
constancy is form

i will build for us a table of words
if you will join me
in honest praise

+

i trailed the previous husband
to the crossroad
and placed a rose-coloured
pebble in a tonsure of weeds

the concrete post
preserves the names
of men and boys
born to girls

in the village below
were they betrayed?
how were they not?
from the skin

that enclosed them
to the spire that
impaled them
to the perfect city

that awaited them
on the night they
were butchered
they anticipated

no quarter. i felt
a cold gust rising
from the river
why did he bring me here?

+

the summer we sang
"The Grand Old
Duke of York"
from Paris to Avignon
and back again
to calm the baby
we passed a night
by an ancient well
in a stone house
that leaked no light

at daybreak, with
swallows
in the fields
i walked down
into a wooded gully
below the house
a stillness there
as if something
was drawing in breath
then i was among them
a throng
the battle clamour
of terrified men
charging and
hacking
weapon clang
on weapon

the terrified foe
crying out
spirit men, at dawn
crashing to earth
behind a village house
owned by the photographer's sister
in Toronto

leaves in that forest
renounce decay

+

i ran the high places
with my weapons
pursuing ibex
i know this grave
my brothers plundered it
we slew the sons
of its occupant
he left us in peace

i claim a home, a remedy
in this sharp, clear light
and in the eye
of my adversary
his wells are dust
the hillside is mined
the young man in that border post
will not hesitate to shoot
no good will come of it

Hugh M'Diarmid's first appearance
in his new skin, the year
Blackshirts entered Rome:

> *An' I thocht o' the last wild look ye gied*
> *Afore ye deed!*

radio transmission in Germany
began the following year

Günther Anders feared that
what would be lost to a listener
would be the *self*
opening the door
to *the inhuman*

Stein in Bilignin, Oct. 1939
... since the war
I have heard the radio
for the first time
and that as the creation
of a modern world
as it is ...
destroying even the present
with which I was at one time
in contact ...

Freud just disliked
the radio

as a student at Yale
American economist Irving Fisher
rigged up an ingenious
hydraulic model
of the economy
with hoses and belts
and later invented
the Rolodex
on his 1922 transatlantic radio broadcast
he declared *the whole world*
a neighborhood
as the first president
of the American Eugenics Society
he lobbied successfully in 1924
to bar all those he called
the extremely unfit
meaning most of eastern
and southern Europe

on his return from Moscow
Antonio Gramsci won election
to Parliament
within two years
he was in prison

why did Pound prefer Italy?
he believed that with
an authoritative government
it would be easier to make the experiment
of his economic system
by buttering up the Duce
he'd speed the demise of
the great forces that have
no visible face.

on May 4, 1938
as Kurt and Arlette Seligmann
packed for a summer in Hazelton
eighty-five diesel submarines
dove simultaneously, in formation
into the Bay of Naples
rising up into their own foam
like synchronized swimmers
they loaded their deck guns
and, in unison
fired off a window-shaking salute
no smoke, no mirrors
the guest of honour, Adolf Hitler
was unmoved

ibex spot you
long before you close
your door

+

we led them to the woods
two big grade-eight guys
from Cornwallis Junior High
they scrambled up the planks
to our tree fort
what did they want
from two grade-six guys
on the far side
of the cemetery?
we lit an impressive bonfire
i gave them cigarettes
(that may have been it)
we stared at the fire
it grew colder
i revealed my plan
i had two songs, i explained
as if they were record producers
men with connections
in postwar K'jipuktuk
scouting talent in the bush
along the tracks
between the graveyard
and the new subdivision
off Dutch Village Road

i can't recall the second tune
it was complicated
but i had a good feeling about
"Juke Box Rock"
"Let's hear it," said one of
the record producers
lighting another cigarette
i began to jerk my hips
"*Juke box, juke box, juke box rock,*
Juke box, juke box, juke box rock,
Juke box, juke box, juke box rock,
Juke box, juke box, juke box rock."
i stamped my feet in time
the smoke from the fire
blew into our faces

"That's it?"
he reached for my pack
of Matinées.
it began to snow

+

only months after Hinmatóowyalahtʼqit, or Chief Joseph
approached the howitzer at C'aynnim ʔAlikinwaaspa
with a cease-fire
Walt Whitman
whose spirit was one with Miss Emily Carr
stepped out of his Pullman
onto the Great Plains
at the waning of the communal
and the waxing of the Individual
a suicidal delusion Melville portrayed
as a self-inflicted con

Whitman took a shine to the cowboys
        bright-eyed as hawks, he wrote
        My days and nights, as I travel here –
        what an exhilaration!
an exhilaration lost on me
on these occupied territories
where illumination
is by gaslight
i'm sorry to be so blunt

here is the botanist Joseph Banks
of the Lincolnshire deer parks
and no stranger to the Hellfire Club
observing the Beothuk
in his Newfoundland journal
aboard HMS *Niger* in 1766

> *Our people who fish in those Parts*
> *Live in a continual State of warfare with them*
> *firing at them whenever they meet with them*
> *& if they chance to find their houses*
> *or wigwams as they call them*
> *Plundering them immediately*
> *tho a Bow & arrows & what they call*
> *their Pudding is generally*
> *the whole of their furniture.*

Olson, finding his voice
in the laid-in poem in "*West*":

> *That there was a woman in Gloucester,*
> *Massachusetts, whose father was a Beothuk*
> *"Red" Indian (her mother was a Micmac.*

portraying the vessel she
ventured in as a girl in 1828
as *an instance of the Pleistocene*
"boat" as such, binding Newfoundland
to the ancient shallops of Biscay
though i detect an anachronistic ur-boat
with the scaled-up dimensions
of a human cranium
an American scalp

bearings only, *svp!*
resemblance is erasure

> Olson: *I've been absorbed by the subject of*
> *America all my life.*

some days it seems that *America*
is the only idea in the world –
a cannibal necropolis
swallowing itself

beneficiaries of the butcheries Banks details
fish the gash that wedges open
the continent
on the holiest day of the year
they descend to the creek
at first light
to bottle the tears of
He who was twice lifted aloft
the second time
by the grace of God
in the arms of
six-winged
seraphim

Das ist Karfreitagszauber, Herr!
the old knight shoos the fool away
and bolts the gate
he confiscates the arrow
or does he?
and was it a swan
or a man
unaware that he is a man
and that he is without
a name?

i hear the convulsions of
Chagall's wounded bird

in the Caribou
ranchers fire up the Bobcat
to disappear house pits
and scrub creeks clean
of weir stones
scattering rocks
where sound figures in water
shape compression waves

that catch the sun
miracle enough
this transmutation
a light pattern, fire-writing

in Enid Stuckey's snapshot
Nora Guernsey hangs up the laundry
on seized land south of Tk'emlúps
I'd do it all again, she tells me in 1975
the hillside where she was happy in 1914
is now trenched by gaping, seeping
ditches for a tailing pond
Apollinaire at Easter the year before
overcome by the phenomenon of Picasso:
... the world is as he newly represents it.
An immense flame.

the present as an invitation
to a bottle of gasoline
from those who pump and sell it
a wily Prince sows
chaos and disorder
until his subjects
beg for intervention
immolation purifies
apotheosis mystifies

i shut my eyes and hear
sound figures in water
Moniack, Jericho, Kingsmere, the River Wye
kneeling at the streams
of my childhood
(Fountains of Youth
made with pipes and cairns)
it is as if i am listening
to myself
from inside myself

water teaches love
as a mayfly instructs a trout

as for the scattered weirs
we'll abide until
the singers return
and they will return

+

arriving at the psychiatric hospital
at Blida-Joinville in 1953
Frantz Fanon happened upon
patients tied to trees.

> *Everyone*, he wrote, *is already tired.*

ethno-psychiatry had flipped *the primitive mind*
onto its nose as if it were a seal's ball
incarcerating patients in institutions like Blida
to reinforce the symptoms
it anticipated and, predictably
detected in Algerian patients –
loneliness, ennui, psychosomatic manifestations
of Europe's *ardour, cynicism, and violence.*

> *Every time we abandon an attitude of*
> *understanding and adopt an attitude*
> *of punishment, we are making a mistake.*

what gives a man the right to punish another?
he is not born with that right
but an institution will reward him
absolve him, and shield him from
charges associated with criminal acts
committed in its name, until compromised
then he's eliminated.

Fanon's patients longed to
hear the Angelus
Algiers was 40 km away.

> *Daily life is set to the rhythm of*
> *a number of sounds and the church bells*
> *represent an important element*
> *in this symphony ... Easter arrives,*
> *and the bells will die without*
> *being reborn, for they have never existed*
> *at the psychiatric hospital of Blida.*

within two years he was treating
fighters on both sides
coaching young men of the FLN
to appear disengaged and nonchalant
in public places
before an action.
their arms, abandoned
at the Bay of Pigs
by fleeing *brigadistas*,
were a gift from Che.

+

by dray the stone was exhumed
and hauled to a snowdrop patch
in a perennial border at Moniack Castle
near Beauly
the outline of a man in a tunic
is graved on one side
his long nose, a lichen
meadow in a pollen hurricane
is code, his club's inverted
which may tell sojourners
lay down your arms
and you will return
to your woman
without misfortune

feral boy in a honeysuckle cloud
with filthy fingernails
i dodged my cousins'
bows and arrows
do you recall Guy's little son
in *Les parapluies de Cherbourg*
wearing a war bonnet
in the blizzard
when Geneviève pulls in for gas?
a similar headdress bound my cousins
to a Canada of totem poles
Mounties, and a log house
where their grandmother Nora

hangs their mother's nappies
on a line

i ran down from school
with an incantation
in the shape of my mother's body
sunlight leaned over me
i read, *Pat sayed tae mither ...*
behind us, the kitchen's
black mouth
the outer door
said Yes
the inner door
said No

we foraged in trees for leaves
in furrows for turnips
a silver-skinned caravan
gleamed
deep in the forest
and was sucked away
by night

in the family beds
militant desperation

the War, thought Nora
had valour, courage
and gallant men
who dressed for dinner
and sacrificed their lives
for God and country
we knew who we were
then everything changed
a pestilence
invaded our homes
before the War

one did one's duty
behind closed doors
we knew all about it
but men became unhinged
women too
they lost their senses
it was shameful
disgusting filthy beasts
ruined our happiness

Picabia on his war experience:
I was bored to hell.

Cendrars on the radio:
Humanity lives in its fiction.

+

he explains that when the Royal Engineers
appeared on the front line
everyone was sworn to secrecy
a euphemism was devised
for the canisters
although the ***
was an open secret in the mess
in the ranks
and apparent to nearby
French villagers who
he relates, were as
hostile and resentful
toward the English
as the English were to them
they *returned our loathing*
he recalled

across spools of razor wire
the enemy observed
the excavations

on the morning assigned
the air was
Dead Calm
against all reason, the order
was shouted down the line
"Open the cocks!"

+

Make of my head a prow ...

—AIMÉ CÉSAIRE
RETURN TO MY NATIVE LAND (1939)

on flaps of sucked rock
and barnacles
you may see airborne grilse
twisting off parasites,
a grimy fan of quills
rocking in foam

pivoting on chains
astride their own reflections
whose footsteps echo in these hulls?
children are asking
will he be coming home
today?

+

a baptismal font
in our hallway
Bedford Basin
from the air, 1943
the convoy's disposition
is reassuring
abstraction is order

> *Mak ready, mak ready, my merry men aw!*
> *Our gude ship sails the morn.*

be a gentleman
my father said
act in good faith
do your duty
dignity and loyalty
are their own reward
may i put it this way
the comrades in whom
he placed his trust
betrayed him
and broke the
heart of a man
born as *The Red Flag*
rose in Berlin

Red Ensigns harrowed the inlet
on white *Empresses*
white into white
carrots of Empire
engineered for luxury, pacification, and greed
in the Officer's mess: R.N. Reserve
Chinese seamen messed below
above them, six hundred
steerage bunks
and for good measure
on the upper deck, turrets fore and aft
for 4.7-inch Armstrong guns
warehoused in Vancouver and Hong Kong
in 1923, bound for scrap
the *Empress of Japan*
billeted scabs
to crush workers
on the Vancouver docks

on this shore
my father
began to misplace
the names of things

> *Half-ower, half-ower, to Aberdour,*
> *'Tis fifty fathoms deep ...*

+

Françoise Gilot recalled the day in 1946
when Picasso, leaning over the balcony
of the Villa *Pour Toi*
spotted Breton newly returned
from Manhattan
down he ran: *André!*
Breton pulled back
repelling the Stalinist hoof
of Apollinaire's flame-thrower
a man outrunning a brush fire
does not stick his fingers
into the inferno

Picasso: *Friendship should be above*
any differences in our ways of
understanding historical reality.
Breton: You must choose;
the Party or me.

that spring, as her health declined
Gertrude Stein bought a new car
Picasso was critical
Why buy a new one? he groused
It's what I wanted and I've gotten it, she replied
So good-bye Pablo.
and that was that

the bull received no quarter
from the foe of Éluard
late at night
one could find him reinstalled
on rue Fontaine
unpacking crates
turning his mind
to the spirit lives
of America

+

and you, Aragon?
you slipped up with that dumb sketch
of the deceased mass murderer
on the cover of *Les Lettres françaises*
the comrades had a fit
what were you thinking?

at first it resembled my father, said Françoise Gilot
the Spaniard drew another, and another
his heart was elsewhere

appetite, appetite alone
not for him sleepless nights
in the meadows of delusion

+

assailed by phantoms
without comfort or succour
an anguished voice cries out
from the sidewalk below

what wisdom is that which
devises as an act of human charity
the infliction of scarcity? next time
i'll take the elevator to plankton

+

on Roussel's syntactical Möbius strip
you'll find fancies
of colonial predation
verbal sedation
irresolute vowels
toggled homophones:
exotic – *erotic* – exotic
the text smacks of paradise
after plunder

a perambulation on the perimeter
of the Villa *Locus Solus*
uncovers verbal wonders, bird
thunders, epistemic sunders
hailing the impossible
as the promontory of a possible
that recedes
as one approaches

the preprandial delegation
encounters a statue of
a naked child, its hands lifted
in supplication
un ancien fétiche africain
intones Martial Canterel
maître de la Villa Locus Solus

the figure, *le Fédéral*
graced the square in Timbuktu
during the reign of the ailing Queen Duhl-Séroul
according to Ibn Battuta of Tangier
so the guests were led to believe
by their host and their host's host
the wizard Raymond Roussel

i have witnessed the fate of nations
confides Martial Canterel
order is vapour
when the throne is weak
shadow dwellers pitch stalls
in daylight's glare
vultures fatten in the lanes
citizens bolt their doors
so it was in Timbuktu
with the Queen confined to her chamber
civility wasted away

one bleak morning
with birds falling from the sky
and horses half-asleep
a green shoot pierced hardpan
at the foot of *le Fédéral*
by noon it had eclipsed the child's nape
(is it true its shadow scored the square?)
unfurling, at sundown
a delicate campanulate bloom
it was a sign

the physician sent for water
from a glacial cascade
carried aloft at dawn
in a crystal flute
by bluebirds

wasps flew interference
over cracked earth
to the royal compound

gently, he steeped the petals
stirring with a gazelle horn spoon
so as not to bruise the nectar
semen-scented, pale as
November mustard
the infusion revived the Queen
whose triumphant apotheosis
on the palace balcony
caused spent vines to blush
their rosy tips
rekindled commerce
trees bloomed
children giggled
traders sent for young camels
birds busied themselves with twigs
to paraphrase Ibn Battuta
according to Martial Canterel
as relayed by Raymond Roussel
in 1914
the year Enid Stuckey
with her new Kodak
snapped her school chum Nora
my grandmother
pegging up laundry
in a little gully on Secwépemc territory
transferred by the CPR
to a young white man who agreed
to break the land

on the far side of the river
among sage thrashers and aspen
Père Le Jeune was building
his New Jerusalem

it had been twenty years
since he'd rolled out his first newsletter
a poorly gotten up thing ...
on the Edison mimeograph

> *Alta naika tomtom aias tlus naika iskom*
> *naika mashin, pi mamuk pipa kopa msaika mashin.*
>
> Now I think it would be wonderful for me to take
> my machine, and write a letter to you by machine.
>
> —January 15, 1892

Papa Pir Lshyun was a companion in Christ
of hereditary Tk'emlúps te Secwépemc Chief
Louis Clexlixqen, or Petit Louis
who four times rode the sleeper to Ottawa
to argue his people's case before the Governor General
with no success in that joyless capital

in 1904 Lshyun set off with Petit Louis
and Spaxomin Chief Johnny Chillihetza
for Rome
and an audience with Pius X
who was, wrote Apollinaire
L'Européen le plus moderne

> was there a vision of a Papal Mandate,
> a Principality of devotion,
> sobriety, and Oblate law
> with Pius X bejewelled and enthroned?

at Buckingham Palace the Chiefs begged Edward VII
to honour his mother's vow
to restore hunting and fishing rights
and title to their homeland
rendered in a recent provincial report

on resource extraction as being
agreeably timbered with Pine and Willow
to no effect

in Europe, they demonstrated mastery
of Duployan shorthand
at a single exhibition winning three gold
and five silver medals between them

for years Petit Louis fought
to recover 103,000 acres
seized by the colony of British Columbia
in the courts and legislatures
of a nation that infantilized him
in the monstrous palaces of a continent
unmatched for imperial barbarism
no one lifted a finger

wearing the antlers of his clan on his cap
my grandfather left his homestead in 1917
to reclaim Roussel's France from the Hun
to restore the territorial integrity
of a sovereign people invaded by force
it was a long way to go to right a wrong
buried up to his neck by a shell
he limped home to the small, dark cabin
and walked out with three babies and a wife
leaving the quarter section for the bank

Canada shipped wild horses to Vladivostok
in 1919, and boys to harass the Reds
but saw no need to raise a regiment
for the repatriation of Secwépemc land
no troops rallied in Liverpool
to press the case for restitution
none who'd shipped out to restore
the dignity and honour of France

could conceive of fixing bayonets
and shelling the Legislature in Victoria
from field-gun positions on Fort Street
to secure the territorial integrity
of the Secwépemc

now a car lot sits on the polo pitch
the root cellar is a nail bar
stripped of game trails
the stolen land is a cash machine
for dirty money

Canterel, in *Locus Solus*
lured figures back from Death
with an injection of *résurrectine*
and the metonymic brace of language
men whose fear of death leads them
to annihilate their Mother
in onslaughts of rapacity and speculation
have no appetite for redress

what did
my grandfather
know

of Louis Clexlixqen's
resolve?
very little

i warrant
with three infants
an older brother

lost in Flanders
the topsoil
as dry

and thin
as a dish
unfit

even for hay
and an intimation
dawning

that something
was not
right

we don't
speak
to them

they don't
look
at us

we return
the favour
the land

is not free
nothing
is free

we're being
fattened up
they'll come

looking for us
again
one day

our dead
live elsewhere
our people

sleep in fields
of stone
we keep

our heads
down, our
noses clean

we stay on
our side
of the street

these are
the protocols
of occupation

+

in the eyes of General Staff
does a big colonial boy render value
equal to a hay bale?

the enlisted man, i mean to say;
officers, especially junior officers
may be assessed
at a lower rate

+

will vectors of consumption edge into
formal agreements-in-suspension? the
opening line was engineered in a mist
and although reproduced faithfully pru-
dencc might advise an inspection of the
hull and propeller shaft prior to embar-
cation. what was the novel we read in
Fourth Form? *Moonfleet*? breakers and
wreckers! a primer on class warfare
and insubordination for future flunkies

boys, when is a crime admissible, even
forgivable? i don't know, sir. when
you're poor, sir? does this mean that
if you are poor you have a right to
take what you want, then? no, sir.
perhaps food, sir? you'd steal food?
no, sir. and you, browne two? can
theft ever be justified? no, sir. and if
you're hungry? say, a little red apple
from an old tree that's heavy laden?
it might be okay, sir, a little pippin.

and your rationale? it might not be
missed, sir. browne two? i think no
one would mind, sir, if someone bor-
rowed one. borrowed, is it? am i to
suppose that the eighth command-

ment is flexible in God's eyes? He can't
see everyone, sir. some boys might
be sick in bed. He'd be serving them
soup, sir. are you saying that if He
doesn't catch you it's okay? how would
He know, sir, if just one went missing?

Eve ate one, sir. a python gave it to
her. what? do they have hands, sir?
who? what happened? she got tossed.
there was an angel, his sword was on
fire. what happened to Eve, sir? sir,
what if you left your sweater there
by mistake? has God got hands, sir?
will God be strangled by the python if
He nicks an apple, sir? it's His. say
the angel smites Him? if God dies,
sir, will we? by sword, sir, or snake?

+

cycling over the bridge from Larraín's *Neruda*
a portrait of hubris lacking conviction
Birney's wartime English Bay
is a pool of dazzling Mylar
an Ithakē of ghosts
on cannery posts

the bike lane once bordered a bleak
one-storey stucco rectangle
on Pacific with a stuffed
Rhode Island Red
in a window beside the door
Kettle of Fish, the place was called
twenty-four years ago, at magic hour
through a window lit by sunset
reflected off a sliding door
in a tower across the street
i caught, in a glance, the eye of Allan King
waiting for his dinner
a journeyman for hire, paying rent
on two apartments
directing an episode, perhaps
of *Neon Rider*
in his old hometown

a fearless, disruptive scourge of institutions
his ferocious intellect was lost to us
during that decade of self-congratulatory

cultural nationalism
and "emancipatory privatization"
he'd seen more than his share of
supper singers

Kettle of Fish gasped its last
stained and empty, the building
became a hostel for homeless kids
with cracked windows
and a busy back door
he'd have approved of that
i passed by last week
the windows were punched out
the roof crushed in
lamps and insulation hung
from the ceiling and the floor was strewn
with drywall and broken panels
it will be gone now, polluting streams
in cattle country near Tk'emlúps

the paradox of the inconsequential
invests the poetics of the ephemeral
with a dilemma
for the gravitational field of the inconsequential
is tinder, amadou
of an incendiary now
lodged in an enduring apparition
of the imperishable

how i long for another hour
in his company

+

sweat squirts ringside into the first two rows
on wrestling night in Dartmouth
or was that blood
on my cheek

we dwelt below the new span, *asoqommtaqan*
workers showed up at dawn
silhouettes, with heads like pulleys
i saw dead men dangling
from steel wires one morning
after a hurricane, i swear

down the hill in Rockingham
we wrestled like bear cubs
on the linoleum while
Whipper Billy Watson
and Prince Maiava crushed
the dirty Kalmikoffs
flickering in a fish bowl

on the suburban shore of Bedford Basin
we solemnized the sacraments
of headbutt and half nelson

one morning at Sir Charles Tupper Junior High
in K'jipuktuk
the Whipper showed up
to meet the kids in the "polio class"

as they entered their basement room
in single file to shake his hand
i slipped into line
limping slightly

+

in the high country
and the low –
snow

+

has tightened

Handshakes

+

a kipper kept me at the table for an hour
after they'd gone to their rooms
beef i fingered out of my mouth in lumps
and placed like clouds around the plate

by morning
catwalks swing
from the new bridge
silhouettes
bound in steel wire rope
dangle in the sky
in tears, Miss ____
opens her drawer
and straps all the boys
in the kitchen, eating crusts
not a word
a band rounds the corner
playing "Hearts of Oak"
silhouettes clear
the Sambro light
the soul is a torpedo

+

and walked out
without a son in his arms
with feathers & pigments
& useless hoarding
to no end, for no end

at the end, a burnt table
bird's meat, fur
frozen streets
he pushes his bicycle
around a circle
with false solemnity
this man without a son
passing Save-On-Foods
on a foggy, black ice
dimanche, dimanche
avalanche
that word, it leapt out
at him when he was fifteen
fifty-eight years on
it finds a home in his arms

+

here's the arched bridge on a blue-willow platter from *home*
that cracked or fell and was tossed over a bank
winter tides tore at and washed back onto the shore
in syntactic shards –
fern trees, a blue quoin
a poet beneath a willow adjacent
to a pond in a philosopher's garden
where a man is fishing
where i may walk
and sing, or pray

as a kid, waking to shouts, she ran down the beach
with what she could grab
men cruising between the houses, pounding on doors
out in the bay, in her dad's canoe with blankets and dogs
reflections on the water, sparks haring into the night
smoke clinging to the narrows
and for sixty more years, intimidation
on the sidewalks
beneath the flower baskets
in that pretty little mill town

Indian Bologna, According to Curly

stuff ling cod stomach with cod bits and vegetables
boil until cooked
remove from water
slice into one-inch rounds
add salt & pepper
fry gently
serve hot

they will not rest

until they’ve flipped

all the leaves in Vancouver

Vancouver in Translation

Guillaume Apollinaire
Blaise Cendrars
Marcel Thiry

A note on the translations

The three poems that appear here in translation were first published in French and in English in *The Capilano Review*, 3.23 (Spring 2014), in a section entitled "Vancouver in Translation: A Conversation with Ian Wallace." Ian and I had for some time been curious about the "Vancouver" poems written in France during the early decades of the twentieth century. The young city clearly appealed to the modernist imagination for its exotic location and its proximity to Indigenous cultures. Posters and printed matter celebrating the romance of Canadian Pacific's transcontinental railway and its sleek white steamships to the Orient captivated the European imagination and made Vancouver a destination for travellers and dreamers. The city was barely twenty-seven years old when Apollinaire's "Les fenêtres" was published as a catalogue essay for a 1912 exhibition in Berlin by Robert Delaunay. "Vancouver," by Blaise Cendrars, first appeared in *Kodak (documentaire)*, published in Paris in June 1924. Neither poet visited Vancouver. Marcel Thiry may have passed through at the end of WWI on his return to France. His "Toi qui pâlis au nom de Vancouver" ("You who grow pale at the mention of Vancouver") first appeared in 1924. I've included part one only as the city vanishes from subsequent sections of the long poem.

Guillaume Apollinaire

"THE WINDOWS" (1912)

From red to green all the yellow is spent
When macaws shriek in the forests they were eggs in
Pi-hi giblets
There's a poem to be written about the bird with only one wing
We'll send it off by telephone
The trauma of it
It makes me weep a little
There's a pretty young girl among the youth of Turin
A poor young fellow who blew his nose into his white tie
Raise the curtain
And *voilà*, the window opens
Spiders, when fingers thread light
Pale beauty unfathomable violets
We try in vain to find repose
We'll begin at midnight
When one has time, one has freedom
Winkles Lottes multiple Sun Stars and a Sea Urchin sunset
An old pair of yellow shoes by the window
Towers
Towers are streets
Wells
Wells are squares
Wells
Hollow trees that hug vagabond *Câpresses*
Chabins sing songs to die for
To their chestnut-haired *Chabines*

And the wa wa goose trumpets in the north
Where raccoon hunters
Scrape pelts
Sparkling diamond
Vancouver
Where snow-clad trains and night fires flee winter
O Paris
From red to green all the yellow is spent
Paris Vancouver Lyon Maintenon New York and the Antilles
The window blinks open like an orange
Beautiful fruit of light

Blaise Cendrars

"VANCOUVER" (1924)

The clock striking ten is muffled by thick fog that wraps itself like
bunting around the docks and ships in the harbour
The wharves are empty; the city is lost in sleep
We walk along a low, sandy coast where glacial winds howl and long
rollers unfurl from the Pacific
This luminous stain in the dripping darkness is the terminal of the
Canadian Grand Trunk
And these bruised halos in the wind are mail boats destined for the
Klondike Japan and India
It's so dark that I can barely make out the street signs where, with my
heavy satchel, I hunt for a decent hotel

Everyone has gone aboard
The oarsmen bend themselves to their oars as the cutter, loaded to the
gunwales, ploughs through the waves
The little hunchback changes course occasionally, giving the
rudder a push
Navigating blindly by the foghorn's cries
We bump up against the sombre mass of a freighter and on the
starboard beam a team of Samoyeds is clambering up
Streaks in the grey-white-yellow
As if the ship is taking on fog

Marcel Thiry

"YOU WHO GROW PALE AT THE MENTION OF VANCOUVER" (1924)

Part 1

You who grow pale at the mention of Vancouver
It's a very ordinary trip;
You've yet to gaze upon great green parrots
Indigo rivers, or Natives.

You have set sail on many steamers
None of them were even shipwrecked
You sweated, unnoticed, under Stürmer
You were too wise to desert.

It's enough for your fragile pride
To have been a soldier wandering
The sidewalks of unknown cities,

And, alone one evening, in a bar on Broadway,
To have loved the Greenaway graces
Of a German girl with wise, uninhibited hands.

Traveller

Fred, I Am in the Spiritual Bookstore

> "Tell us chief," one ventured, "what do you
> think?"
> "The music of what happens," said great Fionn,
> "that is the finest music in the world."
>
> —JAMES STEPHENS
> *IRISH FAIRY TALES* (1920)

Fred, i am in the spiritual bookstore
please rescue me
the real Jesus, smolt
of strewn Orpheus
who decoded the recipe for eternal life
in the water-writing of Jumon holy men
whose waxy knucklebones sprout hair
in a bejewelled chest
the whereabouts of which are known only
to the matriarchs of an ancient samurai clan
determined to foil rivals hell-bent
on cloning the next Messiah
is winning me over

a synthesized sitar vibrates the speaker plate above my head
i am becoming a better person
through piercing sonic blasts
it smells like Buddha's bedroom
i've channelled Leonard Cohen's sideburns
such good intentions
so many prescriptions on these shelves

for shelving self-revulsion
the home addresses of angels and archangels
Fred, the invisible world is suffocating me
the nation is a charnel pit
i told Peter i have of late been weepy
Fred, on your sleek new Brodie
please rescue me

here's a biography of Simon Wiesenthal
with a red sale sticker
i saw him first in Donald Brittain's *Memorandum*
in Jan Vriesen's studio
on Government Street in Victoria, 1974
Jan was painting
post-parricidal villages
here on a shelf before me
is a gentle poet who extracts
convenient lessons from animals
for example, a setting sun engraves an antique path
through wind-kissed grasses
the animal arrives
maybe a mink
sniffing sky-blue banners of vetch
in a glowing dale, casting shadows
reminiscent of a prayer wheel
as if inhabiting a poem in which
an animal like a mink
appears in furry notes of
liquorice, cherry, burnt coffee
and beaten gold
stitched into the vestments
of the Patriarch of Alexandria
and appears to bow deeply
as an expression of humility
to its Maker
a homily follows

but how about this?
a blind, matted creature
noses through
a rank culvert
inhaling spoor
pausing to urinate
before emerging
only to be whacked
on the head
by a farmer's shovel
while the poet pauses
for a beaker of Pouilly-Fuissé
his lines flaccid, tarnished
with the ferric bite
of faux enlightenment
and the nine-mattressed
four-poster

save me, Fred
tell me red is green
dark is light, the cleaver
bows down to the pullet
Alan Rickman lives!
is that Lester Young?
i remember Jerusalem
gave you the creeps
the other day i rode my Brodie
between two cop cars
one rolled down
his window and called
to the other, "Jumper,
on Granville Street Bridge!"
off they went

the poem is vanity's anvil
i feel a manifesto rising in my gullet
Fred, our freedom dreams

let the jackals back in
please rescue me
my arms are beating the air
like galaga snaanga's
i'm shrieking
oh, but it feels good too
don't save me
too soon

i hear you say
slow down, sip from the rim
of the bowl

Traveller

a strip of red
cedar
thick as a wasp is long
will do
whittle to a small beam; make
two, add two, this time
a forearm-and-a-half in length
the coil of green dynamite wire
from Rockingham Park subdivision
is for wrapping the beam ends
tightly to minimize splitting when
brass screw eyes enter
the wood. split, bark, dress
a new strip, like the first, then two
shorter lengths, whittle to hips
and shoulders. with a fine-toothed saw
halve forearm beams, pare away
splinters, wrap with dynamite wire
the colour of boiled lobster
small brass screw eyes make nice knees

wrap extremities, tack short beams
top and bottom
set aside a small hard apple
link screw eyes, prying open with pliers
hook scapula to humerus
femur to acetabulum, shake loose
pierce shoulder

pass tack through, fix apple
to tack, rotate to find
a persuasive angel
that should be angle
whittle hands and feet
right one bunioned, hook
with screw eyes. jiggle
loose. this one is an oyster
in wood, a holy book
a second self
kindling kin
a migrant in our dimension

i mark the hour in which
i tinker with you
we're only a step away
from the wreckers
you dance jigs, the old ones
that frightened me
i hang you on a limb
i blow on you, you take in air
i am restless when you are still
is it you who'll journey
to the moon for me?
is that a feather on the snow
are those ashes?
errand runner
on your way
i lift you into the air

+

dread of the damp
mound, pinched
trench
i laughed these off

dig deeper
its roots wrists
i called for the hatchet
is that a tremor?
has it passed?
i'm not greedy

dear engine
i'm your stoker
your shovel

In His Fine Hand

in his fine hand, from the freshly milled house above the beach
an elegant, cursive *April 2, 1906*
                                        and canoes pulled up beyond the tide
he may as well be, he could not be more
present, a collarless white shirt
black trousers, suspenders

                                I forgot the amount you gave me for the box
                                but I think I got it in one of my books some where
                                however if you remember what you gave me
                                let me know at once.

a Wild West show is wowing them in Firenze
Prince Arthur of Connaught, his right knee on a blue pillow
fastens a garter to Emperor Meiji's thigh
Joyce in Trieste is revising "A Little Cloud"
and tells Stanislaus

                        A page of "A Little Cloud"
                        gives me more pleasure
                        than all my verses.

it was the year Emily Carr met Sewiṉchelwet in Vancouver
my grandfather was engineering his escape
later on, they said
he was
            never himself again

a third daughter was born in an orchard
in Kelowna, under the Syndicate's immigrant apples

Fancy

today she'd have been one hundred
the nurse looked in at shift's end
and asked

Is the window open?
Are her socks off?

making her ready
she was ready
her song cleared the river
her voice rose over the sea
my mother is snow

and the sexual flower is not less red

in my sleep: the anemone on Philopappou
near the steps to the Mouseion
its petals lifting in the wind

in his fine hand he is courteous, mindful
six dollars is six dollars
he makes the god's words shine
like stones dipped into a creek
he is thirty-eight years old
his gleaner pesters him for the planks
from the old house at K______
he wants the names and stories
from the wife

i want to thrust him
into the world's agonies
i'm the thief
the uninvited guest
the empty vessel

this morning, Blaser's gnarled magnolias
salt wind teeming with generations

the sexual posture of those petals
Lucretius, via Montaigne:

Do you not know that in real death
there will be no second You
living to lament your death
and standing by your corpse?

i tug at words like a feral dog
my subject is only incidentally poetry
utopia, i never loved you
except for those triumphant chords, that anthem!
i'll report that my grandfather's respite
was brutally brief
my mother learned to keep her distance
bewildered

early on there was a moneymaker
it brought in cash like a coal mine
a thief with a spade and a burlap sack
working after midnight
could make a pile in a few weeks
committing the unforgivable crime
veins of sorrow stain these beaches

Marjerie and Malcolm in their shack
on the Inlet
young poets tracked them down
sharpen the knife, they learned
before going at the bologna

a missionary's wife
keeps a tidy garden
and is expected
to set an example

do you see the armature?

there was always someone
watching, someone failing
someone listening, taking stock
                                        deployed

i was beside myself, she said
everything
severs something
from something

a raven's wing edges
into a cherry tree
sunbeams rush
the kitchen range

his fine hand, an anemone
in this gale of souls

The following is a list of his favourite colours: French ultramarine, monastral blue, phthalocyanine green, yellow ochre, pale cadmium yellow, deep cadmium yellow, raw umber, burnt sienna, light cadmium red, alizarin rose madder, light red or Indian red.

—FRED BRIGDEN, recalling the palette of WALTER J. PHILLIPS in DUNCAN CAMPBELL SCOTT, *WALTER J. PHILLIPS* (1947)

Seventy-Four Prepositions

picking leaves from trees, huddled in bushes, wrenching turnips like
bombs from the furrows

across the lane, field rock, honeysuckle, bush scent, a rill for worship,
warships

inside that dark mouth, a diagonal shaft of light

corduroy road, a crumbling foundation, in the corner under new
saplings a canvas bag with pennies – bank robbers' loot!

winching driftwood up the bank to buck, Cowichan vest, charred
fingers, one cigarette then another, flipped into Foul Bay, the foil
twisted into chalices lined up along the windowsill

Atlantic gale, a flutter in the spray, butterfly blown north, clinging to a
rock, "I'm going down there."

my mother in the tub, water slosh, nipples as she turns to me, porcelain

a blizzard, where is Akela? Akela? it's the Battle of Jutland, a boy
seaman remains at his post beneath the clubhouse porch light
beside a mangled twelve-inch gun battery, snow drifts, his father's
headlights in the gale, K'jipuktuk

clothesline from the upper porch i knot around my neck, pulling
tight, to our rivals: what we do if we catch you, to Robbie: "Don't
push, ha, ha," then into the evening air, swinging, jerking, pulling

at my throat, late for dinner, stuffing toilet paper into my collar,
"no, no, everything's fine," blood already blotching through

a hole in the cliff at the Dingle, and in the rock face at Breezy Bay, the
warm egg your grandfather rolled in, Liz, when you were not looking

up on Old Smokey, an iron pipe for yanking on, wasps' nest!

flicker on a lamp housing, BB on the bone of an eye, earlier still, iron
pipes, blockbusters, alleys at the lake, the cry of oars, crouching
at the outlet with funnels, pebbles, pyramids, pushing time away,
burning, burning, the furnace in the cellar

in Granny Soot's long room, the airtight red hot, close to molten, sucking
in air, white paint bubbling pink: Wagner's preferred colour

on the British sub, a knife, his thumb, my thumb, here, give the little
monkey some apple, with its little skull & skinny arms, sailing
under the sea from its submarine pen in England. submarine *pen*

three juncos in three minutes laid out on the back porch beside her dish,
Zorba licking her paw, serving notice

a little dugout for the kids on the W̱JOȽEȽP beach, bleached silver, as if
the sea had carved a cradle, a little ark endowed with symmetry,
harmony, humility, and grace: *skúkum.* "May I?"

William's Lake rowboat, Jill: "Do you know what those dragonflies are
doing? ... They're fucking!"

at Carlyle Square, as the double-decker pulls in, flying off the rear deck
with the men

Mum's in the butcher's queue, her blue ration card on the King's Road,
across from Osbert Sitwell's front door

pulling the chair from under the girl bringing cinnamon toast to our table at Sunday School on Dutch Village Road where the earth became a giant man

every morning, from the clock tower, white doves scatter into the sky as we march onto the square, "That's the opening shot," the guy from CBC nods, "yeah."

slow-motion pitching onto Peach Pit, his gimballed porridge as Mi Amigo flips over the muddy bank at Breezy Bay

treading water in mid-ocean, destroyers drifting, sailors in whalers cradling FNs, little heads rising, falling, in eternity

the tip of the wharf at Playa Bonita beneath a tin roof, under the stars, after rain, first a threat – "They'll slit your throat" – and waking to a Black face, smiling, "Hey, man. My name's Baba. I'm sixty-five, but I'm still nice."

a teacher's tenderness in the park, Puerto Limón, his shyness that evening

a steep hill, a rutted road, a woman in black beneath bundled sticks, "*¡Paz y amor, paz y amor!*" from the pickup hippies

figures of eight and red willow wands, a full moon at Jericho, italics on clear ice, no school tomorrow!

the fighter locks on, up my sister jumps, current rushes me away, i'm tiny, she waves, swim! swim!

on the sea floor, buried in sand, looking up at me in alarm, *my face*, Mahone Bay

Karol Wenek, our Sunday walks along the Richelieu, "*They can't kill us.*"

her face bursting into the light, leaving the old self behind on the
happiest day of my life

and then in my arms, our arms

after the shot, in the ditch, holding my breath

with Ian in the clinker, oars bumping, summer uniform blazing to the
waterline, all along the shore phone calls, alarm, *Vessel in Distress!*

at the border, the sergeant's rage, *el peluquero* said the kid with the
machine gun, a standoff, then a rib-breaking crack, a little dog
booted into the jungle with a chain of tin cans, howling, the
sergeant with his razor, grinning

Sandy, from his bed in the living room, from deep within the pain
medication: "Get Colin a glass of wine!"

one last kiss, holding that dear head in my hands

Liz whispering to me at Pat Bay as we leave her grave: "I'm alright."

in a valley bottom in Colombia, blockaded at both ends, masked men
with machetes board the bus, empty our bags, our mouths of words

icy halyards for fifty years in a cardboard box with smashed frames

with Dave Butcher digging up dogs between the ties and stringing
necklaces, Bone Brothers!

hull jammed with contraband, vomiting Canadians, a mute felon, gale
winds, ruptured fuel line, twenty hours out from Colón, Corjo
with his two-handed *colombiano*, pitch black, heavy surf to
starboard, our unspoken agreement: we do not exist

Walt Kelly at the bar, a mountain of ash, alive and incendiary in Bernard
Fall's final days

on the back slope of Monte Albán, skidding down on clay smithereens;
scooped up by the handful in Petra, centuries of smashed pots below the Crusader castle; a platter of *mensif* for the drivers, a gift from the bride and groom

Panama City paddy wagon, rush hour, making faces through the mesh, no drivers grinning back

while we were in the hall, he flew straight out the open window and through the big firs at the far end of the field

green burlap on log walls at the cabin on the Goose Lake Road; a three-by-two-inch flap in a warped drawer, his silver, engraved cigarette case; cattle steaming in the winter night

Marge, at July's end, leaning on the porch rail with saucepan and a cigarette, "Summer's over, Colin."

a favourite song: "You've got the skin on the outside and the bones beneath; you've got the bones on the inside and the skin on top"

how they left, my dear ones, curled up like leaves

driving to the vet that morning, oblivious, her eyes trusting in the back seat

sleet, the *Saltspring Queen*, a Christmas tree from Acland's, power's out, hull crashing into pilings long after midnight

as Bill Bennett on roller skates, *La Bonza Unchained*, "Everything's mine ..."

back and forth across the seat top, a bantam cock, hurtling down a gravel road in a station wagon now that the bribe is paid

Eddie Donaldson, jazz pianist, by rumour *un maquisard*, entering the class, coming to attention, May 1958, "*Allons enfants de la patrie,*

le jour de gloire est arrivé!" The Ancient of Days, his translucent
skin, fingers resting on my shoulder. Dr. P., how loyalty should be

blood pooling in my lap from my nose at the old Royal Vic, a veteran
unscrewing his leg; the rattle in the throat of a dying man deep
in a panel truck, turned away from the municipal hospital, Pasto,
denied again, more emphatically, the frantic son

rocket radio from Art's Smoke Shop, second earphone soldered on,
WWVA from midnight Ottawa, from Esquimalt, Ira Blue on KGO

ether mask, nauseating circles of colour; a pallid communiqué from a
Scottish lady at the spiritualist church; scrubbing our forearms in
turpentine; Saint Joseph on the stoop

at McDonald's in Panama City with the exiled poets of Latin
America, lecturing them on U.S. cultural imperialism and their
revolutionary duty, but we can buy one coffee and sit here all day,
they say, there are no spies. i have been tailed for days

hop, step, and jump at the track meet in Laval, best ever, landing at her
feet, gazing up, that was not Tina at all

my grandfather's only comment when asked: "It was terrible to see our
men falling back into the trenches ... shot by their own officers."

a missing boy found in the bushes by police, *goofballs* on the Armdale hill

rolling off an underwater rock in the River Eden, dragged under, nearly
gone, the green sweater later mobbed by moths

sobbing before Twombly's *Lepanto* in München

in the car, my father: "I understand you now; you're like my brother."

Effie's Point, late August, stars above, stars below, streaks of shot milt

two of us borrowed for the night in Brucie's cabin on the West Saanich
Road

up at the rink, slapping a puck against the boards, twenty-five below
beneath the Milky Way

a cart rounding the corner, horses on hind legs, my arm, cap, the wagon,
this death lodged in my deeps

nose to nose with a black bear through the pantry screen in South Slocan

"I'm in the phone book," she said

that night on Pender Island, *yes*

i weep now as i could not then

+

who brought *letters* from Phoenicia?
the Caananite
his boulder dark and wet
from the serpent's skull
with its teeth
& cranes' cries
he'll raise a temple to Athēnē

  long chains in unison
  broken, unbroken, broken
  s – k – y

Linos made melodies with his lips
& taught his brother Orpheus to sing
his father, Apollo
strung the boy a flaxen lyre
some say that in a jealous fit
he fetched his bow
and pierced his son with arrows

on the anniversary
of each rotation
we remember Linos
son of Ourania
as the world dies
an ox stirs
in the earth

what you may overlook
his voice in the silver air
cattails ablaze with light
the god's face in the pond
longing for your return
aching to hear you
speak his name

A Bullet

if anyone had asked
i'd say i was innocent
risking sun stroke
on the shoulder
of a country road
near Puerto Limón
where was i going?
i was something
was i present? no.
i had cash
in the sweaty little
money belt
under my shirt
did i hear birds
as i lay in the ditch
waiting for
the next shot
skeletal, delirious
after squatting
night and day
with my pants
around my knees
above the blue rustlers
of Playa Bonita?

mira! mira!
his face is flushed
unwashed
his trousers
the same
he is oblivious to birds' song
he has no tools, no lunch
no one
he is not of this world
he is trespassing
on this earth
he has lost his way
some, for their wickedness
must be released
from their sin
it is not uncommon
their minds have travelled on
ahead of them
the kindest thing
is to pray for his soul
do what must be done
and pray for
the forgiveness
that will surely come

Salt Spring

what did i wear
a fifty-cent Sally Ann shirt?
the hillside
seeped into a ditch
i worked with a Swedish axe
at summer's end
bees nod blooms
here is a photograph on the porch
after they carried everything up
from the wharf
it's her birthday
she is fifty
it is 1945
the boat shed's cooking with clammers
O Vesuvius, do you remember the man
with no legs?
it was as if everything was
perhaps a
it was as if even nothing
was too much

the kids came back
to get the garden in
pulling out a cigarette
the old man showed me his arm
with the dent
from a bullet in 1917
she jettisoned her clairvoyance

but when? i asked
tides carve a bight
both ways

did we sleep, did we chop
down a Christmas tree?
and montbretia, a scarlet sign
of summer's end
one old kid recalls hot bread rolls
with a dash of sulphur
the ditch greens all year
but what seeps up from the earth's heart?
grief
nothing to do but keep going
packing cigarette tubes, refilling
the Medalta crock
not buying more than she
needs for the morning
so as not to alarm her daughter
so as not to appear ungrateful
in God's eyes
on every street corner, she said
a woman with a pram
in widow's weeds
i've found a book conceived
before the recent darkness
utopia without quotation marks
"the chain of memory"
"the House of Life"

he carried a god's name
at the tiller, with the coho running
he was god and man incarnate
fishing for tips till dusk
when exuberant dukes
drained their flasks
an hour south

of a bleak dormitory
designed for the breaking
of children by adults
Canada's contribution to the twentieth century –
to those who witnessed nothing
what comfort did your silence buy you?

he'd sworn it was not his fight
the morning after Labour Day
her son drove into town
who remembers him now?
a scattering of letters
on a chart
she watches the angle of light change
as she reads
when the old man went
she cast his ashes into the field
where he'd fetched the lambs
here's where the dog squeezed
under the wire

Marjorie glides out into *the dam*
a white stick
in a forest pond
she has memorized herself
for the masquerade
the axe slices through alder
pith white
she lights another cigarette

*"i see too much
when i close my eyes"*

Overheard

a bird seeks forgiveness
for a man who has transgressed
the bird makes a model of the man
enters it, leaves a decoy in its place
the bird is seeking forgiveness
for the man's killing ways

the man spots the decoy
and shoots it
the bird hears the gun in the distance
and returns with the forgiveness
to find the decoy smashed

Improvisations 1–12

It may even be true that the predicaments of our time will assume their authentic form – though not necessarily the cruelest – only when totalitarianism has become a thing of the past.

—HANNAH ARENDT
"IDEOLOGY AND TERROR:
A NOVEL FORM OF GOVERNMENT" (1953)

Historical knowledge, at least in the modern west, is founded on the silencing and sublation of other ways of knowing, including communion with spirits and the dead.

—STUART MCLEAN
THE EVENT AND ITS TERRORS: IRELAND, FAMINE, MODERNITY (2004)

1.

It has no sexual guideposts, wrote Dorothy Jean Ray of the seven-and-a-half-inch wooden figure found nestled in kelp on the foreshore at Siqnazuaq by a ship's engineer the year ten thousand human locusts disembarked in Norton Sound to excavate the estuary for gold. It was a predictable, lamentable free-for-all, a carnival of sexual rage unleashed by a criminal Republic. Sorry to put it this way, but they were storm troopers, mercenaries, Arctic death squads scorching the shoreline, ankle-deep in arsenic, poisoning the sea, lording it like grandee coxswains – not expendable lackeys of capital. The ship's engineer, whose name is lost, as if only some names deserve recollection, handed the little human effigy to a colleague in Kenmore, Washington – this before the nudist camps – and a neighbour passed it on, she's said to have said, to Ms. Ray. It has no arms or feet. The face was carved quickly, I'd guess, with a penknife, its eye sockets twiddled by the tip, the nose defined by a whittled undercut. The mouth's narrow trench in the almost circular, chinless head was neatly achieved in brief, clean slices. I'd say this figure is singing. With its barrel chest it could pass for a man or a woman. Or both. Which do you hear? An old check opens at its neck and runs to its groin, where the figure splits apart. It has no ears, or sex. Its source? Upriver driftwood, cottonwood or spruce. Before that, before us, the whittled us, what form did it assume? And its calling, where has it been? Cached beneath a woman's pillow? In a doctor's pouch? A child's fist? Is it a charm, an amulet, a spirit figure in flight to the lunar fastness with its dog packs and eternal snows? The sky's a pillow the Moon lays her head upon. Did it surf the current north? Will it heed our plea for intercession? Was it stashed in a cradle, dropped, misplaced, slipped into a pocket, launched into the lapping waves to seek its own lost children? Were there tears? And its origins? But why the past tense? Why assume its work is done, that it has retired from the river of stars? What of its covenant? Its silhouette, rotated sideways, is a coastline, a headland imprinted on generations. Its solitude is our inferno. It is what we make of ourselves.

A being appeared in bird form, Snowbird, pecking around in the dark for grass berries just over there. Light boomed in, darkness flipped its cape, humans rose from a sunlit patch of nettles and vetch. Those newborns scrambled around like little spiders. Where did they come from? Why? And did they, before time, resemble something else? What is their purpose? Form finds resolution in the invisible world. The visible world is a masquerade; on its fields of combat we love and hone our lamentations, but what are we? When pack ice broke up and waders blew in, men and boys returned with their tools in Dorothy Jean Ray's day to Ugiuvak to manufacture geese from whales. In 1955, the settlement was a drift of shacks without running water a crow's mile from the cheerless American grid of Nome. A father who'd left his family to grind out souvenirs on the floor of a Quonset hut *qasgi* for tourist greenbacks told Ms. Ray the old guys *used to drill a hole under the tail of a fox or wolf, but the missionaries told them it was wrong, so they stopped.* Once again, that frenzied mandate, that race to pre-empt the Enlightenment's penetration – in this case of the North – to mortify holy flesh, to reduce the wild, beautiful, subtle body into a filthy shack built in misery for incineration by fiends. Make more, the knick-knack merchants cried, highball it, cut corners, carve faster! It was a crash course in commodity fetishism and compulsory imprecision, in making things that are not what they are for people who can't tell the difference. But if you cannot say what's missing, you must be missing that thing too. You come into this body and this country and pretend to be what you are not and cannot be. That little hole is why men and women prosper. It is where a hunter enters with his skinning knife to discover himself within. Would a god plug the world at one end? He would be a fool. He must hate the world. He must fear his creation.

2.

Comb-over guys in the parking lot at the Edgewater Casino, jingling toonies in their pockets, in expensive shirts and cufflinks. They flip their smokes away; their eyes say, "Piss off, don't judge me." A pair of crows observes a small dog crouching outside the firehall at Tenth and Granville and minces toward the deposit. Our crows show up in early spring to case the lane, sort grass, snap off winter-killed twigs and stack them in the forks of regimented cherry trees. A friend prefers the mall, he's a regular in the new moon of plastic lawn chairs orbiting the lottery kiosk and tube-steak steamer. Over/under, point spread. He's winning big. Auguries of Ithakē, of wild surmise. The drive to San Francisco leads through narrow, terra cotta canyons. Soot falls away, we see half-legible symbols smeared in grease and red ochre. In the old quarter, soft brick warehouses crumble into charred timbers. Façades are ground to rubble. A meteorite has levelled the square, and under the mounds there's a scattering of what are called – in an effort to drain them of presence, of their particularity, of their aura, to scrub love and triumph and fear from their making, to monetize and isolate them from their makers – *artifacts.* I'm the pilferer, the hoarder, believe me. The poet's renunciation of culture in favour of nature, mused Lévi-Strauss, enables her *to discover or perceive properties of the object which are normally concealed, and which are the very properties it has in common with the structure and functioning of the human mind.* Our crows scout the nest in the next-door holly; twice their fledglings have been seized from this tree, plucked, and eaten to the knees by raccoons. In March we defer to the ancient alliances, the predatory nations, to song, tattle, snap, and sudden hush in the garden, to avian grief. Slugs have vanished, and bugs. Barn swallows no longer swoop between the mays; there's not a single sun-struck, dizzy hatch beneath the blossoms. Swallow sister, swallow brother, you'll go hungry on our street. From garbage tip to battleship, only some of this is dream.

3.

I have found my way to the garden; nothing is familiar. The lilac I planted twenty-five years ago bends away from the absent *ombre* of the cypresses next door, its trunks hurl runners into adjacent beds. Heading and trimming ahead of the smoke, I glance down to see my father's forearm, pale, with dry flakes and teredo veins. One day this pruning saw will be as dull and rusted as his was. Micro-particles of torched larch, ponderosa pine, and bone ash sting my throat; the city has surrendered to what it can't run from. I walk to the bus stop at Broadway and Stolen Land where a young woman, clinging to a tree, her face pressed against the bark, sobs in loud bursts. A packed satchel's on the grass. Would she like me to stop? These root-heaved sidewalks are blood diamonds. Shut your mouth; take your cut. Nothing of beauty will come of this era, nothing that is honest or fair. We've been had. The capital that never sleeps has found out our crimson bed. It was a targeted hit, a criminal bloodletting, and how does this narrative include the Old Man, my great-grandfather, who showed up here, they say, with U.S. dollars, having profited from the consequences of a freak blizzard in Nevada? The prairie he acquired was unceded land. When the smoke lifts the con will be complete; when you wake you will remember nothing. I think of the *Essais de reconstitution d'objets ayant appartenu à Christian Boltanski entre 1948 et 1954*, molded from plasticine: approximation as surplus, as its own subject, fully charged, an unforeseen glory, as a mane is to the wind. On the Frazer, Company men watched Stó:lō haul in sturgeon and got big ideas: *isinglass*, a cash crop. Beavers were toast; the HBC had sewn up the salmon trade. On the Sabbath every other chancer was deep in the toolies chipping for coal, dreaming of pre-emption. To the east, rebellions; colonial nooses tightening. In Lax Kw'aalams, *The Sympseyan Indians arrived with potatoes for sale, from Queen Charlotte's Island.* This in 1834. The following year, October 3: *Bought 136 bushels potatoes of one party of Sympseyans and 306 bushels of another.* A year later, Haidas sold the occupiers eight hundred bushels. Their plots prospered; Ireland's withered. Thousands lost their minds, in rags, on the roads. Henry David Thoreau, a Harvard grad who'd sown a row or two of seed potatoes, warmed a cannonball in the fire until it was red hot and planted it in his room to heat the cabin during that first winter. *I had in my cellar*, he wrote, *a firkin of potatoes, about two quarts of peas with the weevil in them, and on my shelf a little rice, a jug of molasses, and of rye and Indian meal a peck each.* He liked spotting, and being seen to be spotting, and pouncing on, arrowheads, boasting of his psychic gift. In the Pribilofs, indentured Unangax̂ slaughtered fur seals for their penises, leaving carcasses to rot. Anchored off Saint Paul in 1805, Nikolai Rezanov found the stench unbearable. *Before I arrived 30,000 male seals had been killed in a single day*, he wrote. *Their pelts had been discarded.* Terrified hunters threw themselves at his feet. He observed in their eyes what it was to be *both Tsar and God.* Brutalized, robbed, and enslaved, the hunters had been forced into a killing frenzy to win his mercy, packing holds with sacks of sympathetic magic to kindle the fickle loins of Zhōngguó. The seal herds collapsed. The slaughters moved on; they endure unabated. Can one spot a spike in the late Qing dynasty birth rate? The Daoguang Emperor sired nineteen children; his successors spawned one or no sons. The sturgeon is without teeth. As its swim bladder deflates it sinks to the river bottom to sift through mud and silt. Those who have heard one say a swim bladder sings like a drum. From stacks in the basements of distant museums, what do you hear? Deep beautiful voices. In the empty music store the practice rooms are silent. The air is still, the woman has vanished, the satchel is gone. The sturgeon play in New Caledonia had no legs. A snapshot of Duchamp's red New York door vanishes from my screen, dissolving into Halloween jack-o'-lanterns. I stood outside for an hour; every intersection is a Battle of Jutland. *Isinglass. Isinglass.* The gelatinous membrane fines beers and ales and lifts its host heavenward.

4.

That summer, U.S. trained commandos parachuted into Santo Domingo de los Colorados trapping forty guerrillas of the Unión Revolucionaria de las Juventudes Ecuatorianas, terminating two days of victory celebrations on the mountain. On an August afternoon on Saint Charles Street, in Victoria, in the shadow of Government House, under the blue reflection of the Strait of Anián, I stepped out of a Fiat Spider in a shrunken, wrinkled, khaki midshipman's uniform streaked pink from combat with a dryer. (I burned it to the waterline one starry night in Finlayson Arm.) A woman my grandmother's age approached, bent, apparently, on a forensic examination of the garden. We admired the shiny border of chrysanthemums beyond which stretched the perfect lawns and hedges of what we called Gaga's house where Roger and I slept on the concrete floor next to an abandoned coal bin in the dingy, web-glittering basement and where we shaved with the same blade all month in the servants' sink, being more or less forbidden to go upstairs. "They look nice," I said. My new companion turned, smiled, and sighed the sigh of one who wishes it known that she will never resign herself to an accommodation with universal suffrage. Half-glancing away, and with a more expansive sigh, she declared, "We haven't had good mums since before the war." Her hand shot forward and tilted the flower heads in her direction, one after the other, like a pediatrician inspecting the upturned faces of street urchins. I confess to you, fifty-five years on, that I had not noticed the flowers, nor could I have put a name to them. It was, in any case, code. I nodded, wiping the front of my jacket down. She turned to me, as if preparing to dismiss Thoreau's awkward French Canadian wood chopper stopping by and hoping for a little cheer on a winter night, or Baudelaire's Millet. She looked away, then back again, squinting, and cleared her throat. "Who are your people?" she inquired. You may recall the retribution meted out to the student vanguard of the Unión Revolucionaria after forty-eight hours in the clear Andean air. You may be asking yourself who bankrolled their training, who stepped forward to sell them arms and combat aircraft at favourable rates, and why? What did their futures hold? Who were their people? As for the chrysanthemum gardeners and their people, where did they disappear to? I think you know. Was she playing dumb? Perhaps you are reflecting on the want of revolutionary discipline and the fatal cost of political deviation detailed in Lenin's *"Left-Wing" Communism: An Infantile Disorder*. The impatience of the guerrilla youth was understandable, even admirable, but foolhardy, a textbook example of terminal error. I stared at the petals. They seemed okay. Had it not been me, with sweat dripping down my back, but a young, beardless sentry, and had she been led, blindfolded, deep into the razor-peaked Venezuelan cordillera, to his camouflaged HQ, how might the Commandante have replied? "*Señor Bravo, my good man, tell me, who are your people?*" He'd respond without hesitation. "*The masses*," he'd say. "*Revolution is water gushing out of the ground*." Sunset was glinting off Gaga's gables in the city of Amor De Cosmos. Swallows sipped from sprinklers on the lawn, little wings caught fire in the air. My mother worked underground in London during the war and was once approached by an unfamiliar man. She and her colleagues had been ordered to take a different route to and from work each day. Was she being followed? And for how long? Had she been careless? Bound by her oath of secrecy, this is as much as she ever confided. I looked down at my scuffed, unpolished shoes, the pink, rippling trousers. My interrogator was waiting. I spoke my name. She glanced up, made a brief calculation, and shook her head. "I'm sorry, dear," she said, and smiling tightly, turned toward the vice-regal residence.

5.

Multiples, shiners, bobbins of the sea, weavers, souls as waves! Wiggling blennies and eelpouts. Cusk-pouts and gunnels. Belted blenny; Rock blenny; fugitive Black blenny with your eye band, huddled under boulders as the sea's sucked out; cirri-prickled Ornamented blenny; Decorated blenny with plumose cirri: Mr. Spencer, a white man, captured you in 'Y̲alis in 1890, at fourteen and a half inches, and donated you to the Provincial Museum; Saddled blenny, taken by Lieut.-Col. Hawkins on the steam sloop HMS *Plumper* in 1861; Bracketed blenny, hauled aboard the tug *Albatross*, a former Royal Navy torpedo boat, in 1903; Fucus blenny, yanked out of a cormorant's neck near Victoria in 1936; Pen-point blenny, transferred from the hold of HMS *Plumper* to a drawer in the British Museum on her return, a bequest of the Lords of the Admiralty; baleful Crested blenny of freshwater stream mouths, hooked by Hawkins under rocks along the foreshore; Wry-mouth, three feet long or longer, a white man hauled you in at Gwa'yi from eighteen fathoms in 1881; Red Devil, with your eyes of the ancient ooze, plucked from a cod's stomach by a white man near Pender Island in 1934, your veins beneath transparent skin; Y-blenny, mini-philosopher, for decades the first member of a blenny triad in the Nanaimo collection; Eel-blenny, in a bouquet of sea worms, pulled to the surface in Esquimalt by Capt. H.E. Nichols in May 1882; White-barred blenny, in 1941, collateral damage when shrimpers trawled Burrard Inlet; Long-snouted blenny; Quill-fish, lured by lamps and torches, taken at Haystack Island off the mouth of the Nass, a stranger to white men until 1925. Sticks, staves, lingams of the sea! Wattled eelpout, a desiccated specimen at UBC; Short-finned eelpout, a fellow traveller, taken by *Albatross* off Tsa̲xis in 1903, and later identified in a lingcod's gullet near Victoria; Black-finned eelpout, by *Albatross* off Nanaimo, reeled in five nights before the Short-finned eelpout; Big-finned eelpout; Black-bellied eelpout, raised from the bottom, a gorger on crustaceans, bivalves, and brittlestars; Soft eelpout; tiny Pearly eelpout, three centimetres long, pried by a white man's finger from the throat of a Black-finned eelpout in 1928; Pale eelpout; Cusk pout, at one centimetre, netted by an earlier *Albatross* in 1890 after rising from 1,588 fathoms, forwarded to the United States National Museum; Burrowing blenny, pale pink, mauve, pale purple, up to fifteen centimetres long, lurks in tide pools, bores into beaches, hooked by a white man off Estevan Point in 1934, eight years before the enemy rose out of the sea, lifting and falling in the swell, seawater streaming from its vents, to clear and load the fourteen-centimetre deck gun.

6.

Beneath the hatching maples on West Sixth, two nights ago, the temperature licking zero, a car slammed on its brakes, its occupants opened all four doors: transparent wings! A dragonfly! I skidded to a stop. Legs appeared. In the darkness a woman loomed with a pit bull straining at its leash and inquired, immediately, about the black cloud. Had I seen it? The northern sky was black, bloated with hail. "Not that," she said. "You can't see it from here," she said. The dog leaned in and sniffed me. "Here," she said, walking backwards, "no, here." Houses blocked our view. "No," she said, "it's back there." I studied the sky. A peal of laughter from the car. "There, no, there," she said, "no." "Is it smoke?" I asked, wheeling my bike along. There appeared to be a plume of tarry smoke rising from downtown. The dog gave me a cold look. In the *Pseudo-Orphica*, Orpheus instructs his son Musaeus on the nature of God. No one may see Him, he explains, *for around [Him] a cloud has been fixed.* It occurred to me then that only the invisible world can be trusted; humans have not tampered with it. "There," she said, "there!" I looked up. The passengers stamped their feet on the pavement. I recalled Sunday's Metropolitan Opera broadcast of *Turandot* with its appalling final act, in this case with "Nessun dorma" tarted up as a vulgar fascist anthem. Liù, the slave girl, her heart broken by the man she loves, is tortured by the state in the person of Princess Turandot. Fearing the worst, she stabs herself to death. The Princess gets the man. At the curtain call the audience released a sexual roar, hailing the assassins' carnal union. Incapable of rescuing

Liù, or the final act, Puccini abandoned the opera. A quick glance at the *Liebesnacht* was all he needed to lay down his pen. Modernity is the mind recording itself. He despaired. In the final moments of *La fanciulla*, Minnie pleads on the gallows for Johnson's life: ... *una suprema verità d'amore: fratelli, non v'è al mondo peccatore cui non s'apra una via di redenzione!* Wells Fargo called for the noose. With crooks switching to suits, there'll be fewer brothers, more scabs; love will be contingent. Perhaps redemption has never been anything but a cheap, sentimental, theatrical device? Stretched out on top of his chest of drawers, gesturing with an Export Plain, my *companion de chambre* in Saint-Jean d'Iberville elaborated, one winter morning, on why Bishop Laval was not raised to sainthood. He'd awoken, startled, in a coffin, deep in the frozen earth. Though he cried out in desperation it was in vain. When the day came to inspect the remains with an eye to canonization, the exhumers were horrified to see that he'd eaten through his wrists. He had despaired. "Up there," she said. "Look!" Were we seeking an omen, or an invitation? "See, it's long." Clouds raced over the rooftops, opening ragged holes through which we glimpsed the stars. A gash in a mountain of cumulus began expanding and shrinking, a twisting dragon that revealed itself then shrank away into a black velvet sky. Soft flakes of snow began to fall. One of Mussolini's masculinist schemes was to replant the Apennines with trees to alter the climate, producing cold winters to toughen up *our good-for-nothing Italians, this mediocre race.* The dog gave me the stink eye. The woman pointed to a writhing rip above us. "That's it," she cried. "That's it. The black cloud!"

August Salzmann's calotype photographs of the architectural monuments of Jerusalem, 1854: he regarded them as evidence, not art, indicating, in response to misplaced interpretations, that they were "not narratives but facts endowed with a conclusive brutality."

—JAMES S. AKERMAN
ORIGINS, IMITATION, CONVENTIONS: REPRESENTATION IN THE VISUAL ARTS (2002)

The original condition of the earth was quite different from what it is today, when we see it as embellished or marred by the hand of men. The chaos that poets attribute to the elements actually reigns in their own productions.

—JEAN-JACQUES ROUSSEAU
ESSAY ON THE ORIGIN OF LANGUAGES (1781)

7.

Who lies before me, glowing? And sleeping, or pretending to, curled up on a stone tree toppled at Palmyra with pomegranates tucked like testicles between its leaves? The sun is bright. His head pools in his hand. We're meant to think he's a local boy, which he'll be called until he dies, and it's impossible not to wonder if "Anonymous" took more than a technical interest in his subject, lying attentive, vulnerable, pretending to nap in the burning light. Da.a xiigang was in his fifties when this young man lay down for the lens on a white limestone tree to await his master's whim. Johannes Christophorus Schweigger, in *De ortu lapidum* (1665), was convinced that *Stones are generated as plants are ... By virtue of their seminary power, each species reproduces and multiplies itself and it preserves its own species intact and perfect.* As the willow's soul is propagated from its twig, a chip of shale begets shale. How mistaken he was; the soul is promiscuous. Touring Egypt with Flaubert in 1849, Maxime Du Camp polished up a young matelot, posed him on monuments in a fez and ordered him to freeze. If he twitched, he was told, the camera would kill him. *Seminary power.* Du Camp took note of his recalibration. My friend Peter might say these images dismay. Call to mind Richard Maynard, civilian – index otherwise if the standing had yet to cross the channel from Paris – bunking in below decks on H.M.S. *Boxer* (twin screws, four guns, 120 h.p.), glad for a paid gig as official photographer on a British man-of-war. Flogging was in force. Twenty-four years after Du Camp's foray in the Valley of the Kings, Maynard lined up occupants of a Gwa'sala fishing camp on the beach below their shelters in Takush Harbour and snapped mugshots for the first Superintendent of Indian Affairs, Israel Wood Powell, another *hayash-tayi*, who appears to have paid his new wards with blankets milled on the River Windrush in Whitney, Oxfordshire. It's 1871. An anonymous caption was once attached to the effect that those gathered on their beach had *supposedly murdered the crew of the* George S. Wright. Twenty-five years later, on Vancouver Island, Franz Boas will offer a buck apiece for a head and shoulders, his sitters queueing up in their best dresses and suits, hair combed, waiting with dignity in the morning sun close to where they all began. The prints were pasted into scrapbooks kept in a New York vault. Was he looking for "types"? I despise the forgiveness of time. Here, in Maynard's photo on the beach below the camp, you will see a small dog. There's a lady in a missionary's dress. Here a man wiggled his head. There a child sneaks a look from a shelter. And another dog. Here's a lady with no top on at all. This is the record of a crime scene recorded by the criminals. Gone are the lyrical arcs and curls Mexican and Spanish improvers applied to field sketches a century before. A man stands erect in a canoe, arms raised in greeting, reminiscent of a sea bird. He is flanked by canoes, often multiplied by an engraver at the artist's, or Captain's, behest, as in the case of "Port Dick, near Cook's Inlet," in which Midshipman Henry Humphrys's featureless coastal profile is transformed into a teeming tableau of two-man baidarkas pursuing sea otters. It was customary to place the hailer on a vessel's port side, the seaward side, in the manner of the Annunciation. The Welcome gesture is repeated, an archetype of encounter, of sacred promise and confusion. Words echo across water, enhanced by song, soon tempered by guile. Humphrys died of smallpox in 1799. Do pebbles give birth to grains of sand? Did the first rock rejoice in its progenitor? *Lapidem adamantem*, the seedling – "*untameable*," becoming stone in the *panspermic* thrust of divine creation; and who, pray, is the mother? The first man loved his maker, to his dismay. O breech birth of a nation. O Mediatrix! Where are *our* flocks of birds? The Superintendent's inspection was conducted at gunpoint. Unwittingly compromised as witness *and* perpetrator, Richard Maynard documented the epicentre of a catastrophe. The family members on this shore were survivors. Europe – *old nations ... mothers of civility* – witness your future. "E.J. Hughes," said my pal, pulling on his jacket, "I'm certain he had PTSD." Lashings of paint on those postwar canvases, endpapers for an ossuary. And this Maynard portrait on my screen with its thin light? Into a file in a government office. Who does not behave as if life is without end? I want to know who will say, "Welcome home, darling." It didn't take long for the new Legislature to announce that everything on the coast was for sale. Whisky and whoring anguished some. Lord Salisbury observed: *The instinct of the nation will never be content without a share in the booty which it sees its neighbours greedily dividing.* As for regret, or want of a remedy, when were they not tucked into the paint box between ochre and umber? Glint between these rocks – did a blenny twitch? No salve in salvage or salvation. I mine silver in these faces. Whistle stop, have you any spare change? Who was I waiting for? When do we arrive? Palmyra, the tree is limbed. Have you said your prayers, child? And this, from John McLean in 1856, a former employee of the Hudson's Bay Company:

As the country becomes impoverished the Company reduce their outfits so as to ensure the same amount of profits, an object utterly beyond their reach, although economy is pushed to the extreme of parsimony; and thus, while the game becomes scarcer, and the poor natives require more ammunition to procure their living, their means of obtaining it, instead of being increased, are lessened ...

8.

He blasted two rounds from his .22 into the muffler on the new car he received for his sixteenth birthday the spring we mustered in battledress and black berets on the playing field near the exploded ice rink. Hawk-eyed Monty, peering up, toured our ranks with his swagger stick. A weedy crop. I knew the pistol from Sunday morning rat shoots at the Gatineau dump. (*Hair trigger!*) Nearly lost toes twice. Despite the intervention – a work of symbolic reclamation – or perhaps because of it, the muffler refused to backfire. We shouldered arms, lurched right, and stumbled off in last year's sweaty uniforms to hand in our battered .303s. "That's a nice snake I've reared in my bosom," said the Kaiser after the premiere of *Salome* in Berlin, which, in English, at any rate, must qualify as a box of Freudian chocolates. I fear for them now, my old comrades-in-arms. Harm opened wide its mouth. Ten years on, the Geological Survey of Canada compiled a *Catalogue of Selected Airphotographs* without airphotographs. Two bucks. Sun Ra was in the studio with *Atlantis*; Braxton had recorded *For Alto*. I spent the year violently disassociated from myself. Between green bristol-board covers glued over rusted staples, fluid geomorphologic phenomena lodge in austere Courier topographies, striking radical notes of unintended postmodernity and textual evocation, flukes to steer numbed flesh toward phantom shores of acuity. In the pouch: a fold-out map in a red grid with a ratio of 1:50,000. Try these kites.

> 5,100′, *f*/8.14: *Abandoned proglacial lake beaches, spits and headlands. The beaches show one above*

another like contours on the hills. (1931)

9,500', *f*/8: *Glaciofluvial feature, apparently a large radially furrowed outwash fan.* (1935)

Translation? Abstraction? A frugal allegiance to similitude, or the similitude of allegiance? Navigable rivers, strategic bluffs, seasonal floods, defensible meanders: maps are prelude to the kiss of occupation. Monty was milt to us, the coming crop. A girl in the subdivision had a grass snake in her shirt that rose through her open collar the night a hurricane dissolved our hillside. Mud mummified the basement. Flashlights in the dark, fathers shouting through the night, the snake's tongue the next morning, restless on her chest.

5', *f*/60: *Logged hillside, sandy soil, gravel washed away, trenches exposing bedrock, muddy overflow clouding Bedford Basin.* (1956)

We French-kissed in the basement. Who was that? Joe Morello. And that one? Charlie who? In the housekeeper's suite below the stairs, lifting the needle back to the cymbals on "That Old Black Magic." So long, Arthur Ransome; adios, "Invictus." Hello Keely Smith, Ray Charles, Louis Prima, Carmen McRae, Paul Desmond, Errol Garner, Fats Waller, Lester, Duke, Satchmo, Trane, "East St. Louis Toodle-Oo." Jazz cracked me open: jazz heart, jazz brain, jazz talk, jazz walk, jazz mind, jazz skin, jazz cat, jazz chick, jazz street, jazz joy, jazz sky, jazz sex, jazz eye, pre-linguistic, post-atomic, pre-girlfriend, post-puberty, cherubim, seraphim, fire and hail, Adam and Satan, holy of holies, Pastor Fuzz, ace in the hole, Dizzy and Bird and Dave and Monk, and jack knives in our pants. In flood, in flood ...

20,000', *f*/6.02: *Meandering stream in flood. Levees and bars are emphasized by trees standing like hedges in the water.* (1954)

A nation sloshing in stump water, sand banks parted by peaks.
A head falls back.

> 11,500′, *f*/6.05: *Folding and contortions of drag-folds*
> *are clearly shown in steep-dipping Precambrian*
> *strata on a rolling, bevelled surface.* (1945)

Water rising at the jams, everything gives, cutbanks, shores,
cottonwood cave-ins, tangles, bends, prefixes, suffixes, signatures,
blue notes, hi-hats, horns, galaxies of nightingales and stars.

> 20,000′, *f*/6.06: *Braided and pitted outwash.* (1949)

> 30,000′, *f*/5.99: *Abandoned and misfit river*
> *channels (outlined by snowdrifts) eroded by glacial*
> *meltwater streams. Locality is about 40 miles*
> *southwest of the south end of Hadley Bay.* (1958)

> 1,000′, *f*/8.12: *Tombolo formed from a drumlin.* (1931)

And our birds, our darting insectivores, what of their collapse?

9.

Nipple's unrelated to Old English *nypel*, "elephant's trunk." Elephants? Why think only of islanders prying nails from the hulls of *Discovery* and *Resolution*? Their crews were equally eager. How did *trunk* enter English? Through the branches of a tree, that gracious, patient being, glory of the sky, emissary, ally, roost. Cook's regrets were sincere, still, rapacity prevailed, unleashing God-struck fanatics, looters, grifters, messianic psychopaths, and sexual opportunists to plunder and enslave their hosts wherever they put ashore. In Michoacán, commerce with the divine called for infusions of blood and maize. When a warrior was taken in combat, destined for sacrifice, his captor declared, *Here is my beloved son*. The captive responded, *Here is my revered father*. In Tlaxcala, beset by an oppressive missionary gloom, friars were subjected to mock pity for preferring *sadness and solitude* over *pleasure and contentment*. Religious melancholy, observed Robert Burton, is an occupational affliction: ... *where God hath a temple, the devil will have a chapel ... where there is any religion, the devil will plant superstition*. The predator, in his pride, becomes prey, the brooding, melancholy son, object of his own despair – Blake's Urizen run amok. Burton, 1638, on "the melancholy juice": *What makes them so freely venture their lives to leave their native countries, to go seek martyrdom in the Indies, but superstition? to be assasinates, to meet death, murder kings, but a false persuasion of merit, of canonical or blind obedience which they instil into them, and animate them by strange illusions, hope of being martyrs or saints?* In Michoacán, the friars' pallor marked them as the living dead. It was said they collapsed at night into stacks of bones, in which state they descended into the underworld to visit their women. Or were they Tzitzimime, the Sun's mortal enemies, who will plunge from incendiary skies in the final days to slaughter and consume all men, women, and children? In the *Codex Magliabecchi*, the Tzitzimitl is skeletal with raptor's talons and bird's eyes for joints. About its neck hangs a strand of human hearts. Six severed hands dance on his diadem. In a mimetic *bouleversement*, some Michoacáns opted for Lucifer, who offered certainty in return for tribute – a betting man's option. Salvation's a mug's game; but then, a modest investment in slaves guaranteed decent returns and clinched long-term prosperity for a man with a whip. Dispossession, incarceration, slavery, extermination: the foundations, we're told, of civil society. Should citizens be refused the right to exalt themselves with selfies in the gilt drawing rooms of tyrants, in filthy tombs and relic farms, in unbottled dawns on boulevards dark with blood? Machiavelli proclaimed Ferdinand, a murderer, *the greatest monarch in Christendom*. Where might one expect to find justice today? Wherever I look, wherever *those deep, impetuous desires, war, love, and gaming, are in full flood, like Orinocos of the human heart*, cruelty and torture are advanced as God's will. In today's newspaper: dozens of protesters shot dead by the IDF, many by snipers. Twelve hundred wounded. Live ammunition; expanding bullets. A government minister has forbidden students at Bezalel from exhibiting art in protest. An influential buyer thinks an elephant with its face hacked off will speed his foe's demise. Another orders a pouch of powdered horn to revive his sagging dick. Brothers and sisters, peace – the quiet life – is not sufficient. Peace without justice invites tyranny. Hypocrisy is the impacted stool of moral cowardice. Victor Serge, in Mexico City, 1943, alerted to Mussolini's expulsion from Rome, recalling his prediction twelve years earlier: *The Gramscis and the Terracinis know they are almost nothing at this time, that they could be assassinated tomorrow, that they will perhaps never see the light of day, but they understand history's inexorable laws, they know how parades end ...*

Lettre de Paris

For Norman Armour

At night – the furs of Sacher-Masoch become phosphorescent and one sometimes hears from a distance, tired and monstrous, the agonized bellow of the antediluvian monsters of the exhibition of Chicago.

—SALVADOR DALÍ
THE SECRET LIFE OF SALVADOR DALÍ (1942)

10.

The Old World? Really? Does it still romance the cobblestones with accordions and the savage *œil* of André Breton, that enthusiastic name-dropper, that enviously maned projectionist? Though he revelled in the catachrestic japery of convulsing the bourgeoisie, transmuting the predictable into hermetic code, he was rigid as the rails that sped his photogenic coiffure through imagism's timorous eve. He had no ear for music – Offenbach, perhaps – and refused, it seems, to submit his body to the promiscuous, or the irrational, or to any avalanche he could not outwit. The field mouse, on the other hand, was enthralled by Thoreau's debut on the flute; it beat a retreat when the scales became command performances and the flautist's self-esteem became unwholesomely dependent on its cryptic expressions of wonder. Artaud, from Ville-Évrard: *I have often thought of Gabriel the archangel when I watched the face of Breton light up during manifestations of surrealism ... He too will come back to God.* Near the iron tower reserved for the erection of military aerials, a polychromed uterus rises from a groomed forest floor to evoke the confection of *l'état sauvage* where *l'état civilisé*, its eye on immortality, took possession of the spirit beings catalogued and stacked on silent storage shelves far from home. They'll soon be wards of robots. In the gift shop, toys, dolls, bamboo snakes, and in translation, Thoreau's *Journals.* But why here, in this bazaar of Other intoxication? Guillaume Apollinaire, twin to the steam shovels of Panama, knelt before Poe and Whitman; Baudelaire elevated Poe. An embodied high five to militant self-reliance, Thoreau worked up righteous variations on Sam Slick, recalibrating the world in his own annoying image and cadging early dinners at the neighbours. His cabin was an egg that hatched; Henry's the chick who camped in the shell. He had his reasons. Who doesn't? Are they *reasons* though, the sorts of reasons one is alert to, conscious of, convinced of beyond dissembling, as if that can ever be? He rewound the always-unravelling braid of convention, lashing classical analogies to conviction, a shepherd's calendar for a hillside shorn of shepherds and ewes. But how you also please me, Henry, you yokey, sticky chick, how you make me long for your tenderness, your exaggerations, and earnest experiments. Out of yourself you built an instrument, and on that instrument you played yourself and the transcendent promise of shimmering hilltop America, of the self-made, self-contained, self-governing, self-basting, self-detonating citizen, the wily confidence man in the market for market-undermined souls. *That government is best which governs least*, you wrote, as if your neighbours were monsters of benevolence and mercy. But your good fortune, Henry, your *faux* freedom, like mine, came, and comes, at a terrible cost. High-minded homilies numb the senses (sanctimony as history's Zamboni); masquerade veils masquerade veils masquerade, like body checks by an ambitious little god. Henry, you and I are scavengers in scavenger nations with a bent for self-righteous dissimulation. Feast becomes fist becomes fiat. I've shown up for the burst of scent in this wood, gasping for air in the heartbreaking hour before rain, or later, when dusk pries its finger out of the blue eye of day and the pond is still, and dark, and ducks shift their ducklings into the middle, out of range. Says Henry, closing the door, "I am not the King's flute. I am my own flute." And who is this pond?

11.

In 1968, Gwendolyn MacEwen charged the air with magic in an Anglican basement on Laurier West in Ottawa. I think of Cecil Taylor, punctuating phrases with percussive sucks on a cigarette, how, by chance, he came upon Billie Holiday – singing – when he was twelve years old. Bless you, Lady Day, you introduced him to himself. Gwendolyn MacEwen, you emptied me into my body, you pried free my latent voice. And Karl Spreitz, listening to Billie in the sun on the Old West Road when I pulled up in the Green Henry forty-six years ago. "Good Morning, Heartache." Said Ina, "Can you park it on the grass, so oil doesn't pour onto the driveway?" Sun bouncing off green into the trees. Pareidolia. And the yawning heads of peonies this morning. Dianthus. My pores sea anemones, O Adonis, flushed, incandescent. Occult syllables of inner shales, explosive, transgressive polyphonies. Gwendolyn MacEwen, I rose up into my own skin. The sculptor said the mind lives outside the body. This morning, on waking, the words: "I must face it, whatever it is." What can that mean? At the century's end, Chief Johnny Muldoe found thirty-five stone clubs at the bottom of a post hole he was digging in Hagwilget Canyon in the ancient salmon village of Tse-Kya. In those days, Queen Vic ruled rock forms on the White Lake Road. In 1938, at summer's end, in Hagwilget, Kurt Seligmann paid one hundred dollars for a pole from Tse-Kya and shipped it to Paris in two pieces. The clubs are beaked and snouted, with eyes. One is a sandhill crane. In early spring, the cranes drop down into the alkali shallows of White Lake to feed and rest. The pole,

K'ëgit, was raised at dusk outside the Musée de l'Homme in January 1939. In the narrow canyon, Seligmann had admired its patina. *Le mat Keïgiet,* he wrote, *a une belle patine qui varie du gris argent au brun cuivré.* Christian Boltanski thought the Musée a *great morgue.* Are there photos of the assembled guests? The train from Barcelona will soon arrive at Gare d'Austerlitz with worn-out, wounded fighters from the International Brigades. On the southern border, male refugees are being detained and incarcerated in camps. Spanish fascists have taken to the streets, according to the latest headlines, crying "Long Live Death!" What is it that stands in the way of mercy? A new beak was commissioned, carved, fitted, and found wanting. The effect of night lighting on K'ëgit was later described as *saisissant.* In New York that year, Benjamin Britten met Colin McPhee who introduced him to the gamelan and his two-piano transcription. I want swallows to return to our street. Do you remember "Man"? He was, in my childhood, a giant figure of Hope – think Swedenborg's big man of the sky – a cousin of *l'homme primitif,* an Enlightenment Adam conceived for the purpose of masking shame and complicity. Frantz Fanon: *When I search for Man in the technique and the style of Europe, I see only a succession of negations of man, and an avalanche of murders.* Did you notice when the adjective *unforgivable* was quietly retired? Not long ago, excavators unearthed a stone club with eyes and a beak beneath a British tennis court. It arrived swaddled in a blanket. "No idea," said the woman to the keeper. Then she remembered. Canadian troops had bivouacked nearby during the Great War. At night, through glass, from its nest of wood and feathers, it listens to the great winged bulls and the death throes of unpenned lions crashing to the earth in room 10a, bristling with the arrows of the King. In Paris, after Liberation, the Canadian Army enforced Canadian law. "Status Indian" soldiers on leave were forbidden to drink. Cafés, bars, and hotels were off bounds. A Wet'suwet'en woman recalled that the Eiffel Tower was *the rendezvous point for a lot of the soldiers,* including her uncles, who showed up in the evenings for companionship and shelter. They earned $1.30/day. Did they visit K'ëgit at the Palais de Chaillot? When will the invisible become visible? How would we know? Crossing the water on my green Brodie, the air is charged with luminous filaments. Shimmering peaks of cottonwood are spawning; the city is dense with the scent of sex, tree sex. So, *this* is *swooning*? I want this moment forever, I long to dissolve into this moment, to hear my breath, to feel my heart against my ribs, to be a creature among the beaks and bellies building a sky and churning the earth. This galloping spring, its correspondences, its open doors, its aching light, a spike belt in Abbotsford, the half-man on the Bering Sea shingle, the giant, lacerated figure of the cosmos in love with the mind in which it was conceived, the river, the rover, the mother, the infant, the analogical glass in which I glimpses I glancing away, the incantations of a poet in an Ottawa thunderstorm, syllabic sparks, the face pulled aside to reveal faces within. What a splendid masquerade it's been! Look at me: scavenger, speculator, beholden to capital, ripe for plunder, a delusional beacon of probity. Now tell me who's hypnotized by trinkets. About the time that Heinrich Himmler was scouting occupied Poland with the poet, playwright, and honorary SS officer Hanns Johst, a boy named Thith-hak-key – Johnny Stelkia of the Osoyoos Band – inscribed on a deer-hide wall hanging a ceremony from the supernatural world given to humans for the perpetuation of their own. At the centre, Coyote in human form, and circling him, counterclockwise, Turtle, Deer, Bear, Frog, Beaver, three others: Fox, perhaps, with a white-tipped tail, wearing a blue and red blanket. He carries a bag or a box. Frog capers in a cape. On the far side, is that Snake with a horn? He is a horn. All in buckskin save Turtle with his cane. Coyote's jacket is fringed, he wears a war bonnet; eagle feathers fly from his staff. Up on his paw tips, he conducts. Thank you, Thith-hak-key, for your offering, for the cosmic wheel in harmony, for this intimation of eternity, *pour la suite du monde*. I recall the girls in the back seat, gazing out the windows: "Just think, our husbands are out there somewhere." Behold the mercy of the nail, hardened and hewn, its head, its compression of the surround. It is a doubled thing, arm and sleeve, joining by cleaving, itself the apprehension of itself. Spike, awl, stamen, nib, figure of iron. Knowing, or the ripple of vanishing, half-lucid impressions we think of as knowing, is analogous to skipping stones on a belly of water. The surface lifts and moves outward, rising to meet the sun. And the peonies this morning, opening wide. I is multiple, *sans fin*

12.

Able here's unable there. We're in a miniature colonial house off Central Avenue in the no man's land between Phoenix East and Phoenix West; night has fallen. We are speaking of Dorothy Jean Ray and the colour photograph of the Berkeley mask on the front cover of *Eskimo Masks: Art and Ceremony*. That morning I'd walked past the cactus and entered a gallery; there she was, Iralum Yua, Spirit of the Moon–Woman, and her sister, also Iralum Yua, with goggles and tattoos, holes in her ears for earrings. Fresh white feathers crowned the sister's *ellanguaq* – a respectful bid for intercession. I studied the fibres and knots that fasten the hoops. The server refills our glasses. I recalled the Iñupiat guys who came south to Ugiuvaq to carve seals and polar bears for tourists, and the missionary who ordered them not to drill the little anus hole, and how I imagined them shaking their heads as if to say, "What next?" although they knew better than anyone what was next. Children shriek on the grass outside. The flatbread is gone. The server brings two more glasses. I dreamed last night, I said, of *Trois têtes. À l'amitié*, Matisse's drawings of the faces of his correspondent and collaborator André Rouveyre, Apollinaire, and himself, in melancholy three petal clusters, thirty-four years after Apollinaire's death – who can forget his plea to the doctor? – and of how the tenderness, the weight of Apollinaire's hand in his endured, and thirty-four years is a radiator spark on a winter night, and in my daze at the Hampton Inn Midtown, where I believed I'd lost a favourite shirt, the petals became the masks of two girls smiling, posing, squeezing together shyly, before vanishing, and you may think that your days and nights are bedevilled by a boar-headed king crashing out of a burning forest, but he is not brave, he is a fraud, a con, a bloodsucker whose end will come coiled in chains on a hard little square at dawn. What about the guy across the aisle dozing in an NRA ballcap, he must be recoiling from the big gun show. He is groomed; will he choose Blackwater in Syria, or enlist in the president's paramilitary guard, and is it better for a boy to carry an AR-15 or to carve an ivory seal without an anus, and are we not here to open our hearts to the hummingbird, the silverfish, the oak, the palm, the shadowy loner who touched me up for two bucks U.S. at the electric tramway stop, to claw away silence, to admit error, to forgive, to grieve? In Paris the great man raged against his adversary whose hands were skins of fire and light. We are not fireflies, and the night is long and can be bitter. Among the accessions by the Smithsonian Institution listed in the *Annual Report of the Board of Regents ... for the Year Ending June 30, 1906*, E.M. Anderson of the Provincial Museum in Victoria, BC, contributed a moth. H.O. Bergh in Quatsino sent "2 Indian skulls collected in the neighborhood of Quatsino." M. Lewis Crosby in Boston, "2 bullets telescoped in flight." Mrs. E.M. Ziegler, "3 mounted Polar bears." Miss Josephine Marshall, a "Pearl from a common oyster." Ira T. Lee of Thrace, Arkansas, "2 specimens of rat-tail maggots." The American Museum of Natural History, on exchange, shipped "About 500 moths," "2 species of ants," and, on loan, the "brain of an Eskimo." What, pray, was her name, and why was she in your hands, crimped by caliper dents? A voice said: "Let the words speak to you. I am the coil within the coil." Victor Serge, photographed in Wolfgang Paalen's studio in San Ángel, Mexico, in 1942, the world in their hands. Serge, in his journal, recording his wife Laurette's account of Paalen's anguished conviction about the role of art *as a factor in revolution; that is, in the transformation of man. Moral transformation of man is needed, a Picasso as great as a Trotsky*, and Serge concluding, *Picasso? The man is not great*. On the walls of Serge's emigré home when he was a child, *there were always the portraits of men who had been hanged*. In 1916, my grandfather Colin received a telegram: his older brother, in France, suddenly, in the line of duty, the King regrets, he regrets in his counting house all afternoon, and it's not an abstraction, this brother's soul, it has weight, it is cold, swollen, bruised, abandoned to sleet, and lifted by frost. Gertrude Stein will write in anger, *This war teaches us to be certain of our hates. We must clear away boats and hope that somebody is caught ... We must declare magnanimity to be too great a price to pay for self-respect. We must be courageous. We must surely surround women*. In Alaska, Wolfgang Paalen purchased two "prehistoric" fossil ivory figures said to be from Norton Sound, perhaps from Walter Waters in K̲aachx̲aana.áak'w. One, ten centimetres long, has a hole drilled into it; in the cavity there appears to be a pitted pebble, a stone that can be withdrawn, replaced. I thought at first it was the heart, which may be given and taken away. I looked more closely. This cavity is where life begins. Who, pray, is this little ancestress; does she have a name? Did she belong to a girl, a mother-to-be, her attendant? How did she enter human hands and whose hands let her go? And those who hopped, or leapt, or grabbed a hand and closed their eyes and were pulled onto the ice in the North Atlantic, shifting from hip to foot, to watch their ship – filthy, cramped, diseased, seething with rats and lice – go down? After a short time, there were no infants crying, no groans from the dying, there were only the dying, sliding into the sea. In my childhood, *the peace of God, which passeth all understanding* sent us home dipped in the Mystery at the heart of things. Little pebble, new life, one final breath and we vanish into air

Petal

From *Music for a Night in May* (2018)

Petal

1.

what does it want
this body
hung on a hook
it hides from me?

it don't like my looks
we never agree

this body is a jealous god
with an ache for immortality
its surrender is an ambush

a ruse, a ploy

late one night as you sleep
it will open its eyes and whisper
"Petal, i love you,
i prepare you for the end."

half in love, you bend

why me?

a window bangs open
run, Petal
fall in
fall through
farewell old you ...

2.

far, far above me, immensity
the stars go on forever

far below, plumes of smoke
ruins ...
at night the city
bursts into flame
by day, predators
walk the streets
man betrays man
woman runs, if she can ...

down is up
up is down
no north star
no work in town
no compass rose
no rose at all
the bully's in his pulpit
the queen is in the hall

the best jobs round here
are plating the APCs

our strategy?
delay calamity

tread water

breathe, Petal
you are all you were
you were the sea
your feet flow into fins
oh gills!
dive into the pearly night
and swim

follow the tide on wings

let mackerel
be your guide

all night, petrel's
by your side

seas are skies
skies are seas
here steps are swept
by starry knees

look! a light

rocks, trees

landfall!

little ember
bud-to-be
the earth in you
is glowing
rain kisses your cheek

an ancient cedar lifts its wings

pilgrim, you're coming home

in the valley of the clavicle
a wish bone is a bird's phone

your spirit greets a swan
a serpent
a throne
a bear

wearing the crown of creation

3.

rising, falling in the arms of the sea
a masthead light, a bell

oh Petal
how does your coral grow?

desire bends down to caress us
to fetch us from ourselves

picture a boat
like a wound on water
a wing on water
that floats on words

love's mercy
steers this boat

ship oars, and tremble
voyageur

c'est l'aviron
qui nous mène
qui nous mène
c'est l'aviron
qui nous mène en haut

Petal, i spy you
from afar
you are not only

who you are
you sing the feathered heart
of things

with ears for oars

and oats for strings

bend, Petal
in this wind
an oyster
is an antelope
a blenny
in the belly
is the holy child
of an interstellar
smithereen

your bones are carved
from stars

Petal, the invisible work
resumes

pollen gliding
cells dividing
marry the body
and bloom

Envoi

+

white beard
morning legs
Main Street
startled
as a trailer
slams into
a pothole
not missing
a beat
"*Fuck off!*"
he shouts
to all Creation

+

belly of sparks
belly of moon
belly of hell
belly of corn
belly of dreams
belly of squalls
belly of cloud
belly of barking
belly of furrows
belly of unrequited forms
belly of cries
belly of night
belly of blasphemy
belly of Argonauts
belly of Joe Blow
belly of Jane Doe
belly of ice
belly of ire
belly of beaks
belly of stones
belly of spells
belly of coals
belly of oaks
belly of sky
belly of foals
belly of drones
belly of lions
belly of loaves

belly of loons
belly of loins
belly of assassins
belly of spills
belly of sheaves
belly of cuts
belly of doors
belly of smears
belly of irks
belly of thieves
belly of laughter
belly of seeds
belly of claws
belly of mirth
belly of salt
belly of wood
belly of scorn
belly of fur
belly of Jannah
belly of mint
belly of silage
belly of alder
belly of rose
belly of greed
belly of gulls
belly of fury
belly of fraud
belly of grace
belly of larch
belly of sighs
belly of grain
belly of scallions
belly of snores
belly of sunrise
belly of joy
belly of rue
belly of horn

belly of contrition
belly of guile
belly of grief
belly of freight
belly of flight
belly of appetites
belly of beasts
belly of defiance
belly of rage
belly of gristle
belly of peace
belly of madrigals
belly of ardour
belly of longing
belly of birdsong
belly of tempests
belly of humility
belly of witch-hazel
belly of the charcoal line
belly of the leaping up heart
belly of long grass
belly of oaks at dusk
belly of the evening star
belly of the tiny person of bone
belly of the name of the beloved
belly of the song of the beloved
belly of the eyes of the beloved
belly of heart's ease
belly of the beloved
belly of tribulations vanquished
belly of forgiveness
belly of forgiveness
belly of forgiveness
belly of boundless love

+

two balls roll down an inclined plane
imagine a gentle slope on a rock face
in memory's scarred recollection of the Canadian Shield
as they descend, one encounters
an interruption
something imperceptible
particles from a worm casting, say
or a scratch
and veers slightly
slowing down, or accelerating
wheels linked by an axle
find their rotations similarly altered
one will soon swing around the other
gusts produce similar effects
but what might by a fretter be called an impediment
is the *participant*, the third thing!

the participant invites us out of ourselves
into the world
the participant throws open the doors of perception
the participant is Eros and teaches the lover
to cherish the body in song and movement
to hold in memory morning light
on the curtains and frosted windows in Kagurazaka
and the shadows of tossing branches
outside our narrow wooden door
how can i not crack my head on the lintel
when i don't duck?

+

0528. rain. i'm on the fo'c'sle
of the dockyard boat, the *Sine Wave*, on my belly
chin over the side, watching
flounders. we coast above them
they scoot, kicking up sand
with their tails. eruptions, accelerations
the water is as clear
as the songs of Creation. look,
there's another, and another
in the sand, gazing up at me
i know that startled face
                                        then, zoot!
a summer morning
the engine thumps away
                                                        zoot!   zoot!
brothers!

+

that wolf
at the far reach
of the snowy field
gazing back at me

sister!

Notes

Introductory Epigraphs

IX: *One day [Durus] returned in triumph from Batuan ...* Colin McPhee, *A House in Bali* (Singapore: Oxford University Press, 1989 [1947]), 95. The *klian* is the government-appointed headman in a village. A *dalang* is a puppet operator.

IX: *For the story of Orpheus is of the truth ...* Christopher Smart, *Jubilate Agno*, XXIII, lines 52–57, in *The Collected Poems of Christopher Smart*, vol. 1, ed. Norman Callan (London, UK: Routledge and Kegan Paul, 1949), 323–324.

X: *When the films are finished ...* Chantal Akerman, *Ma mère rit*, Collection Traits et portraits (Paris: Mercure de France, 2013).

Diorama

3: *is it not unfolding as we imagined ...* A few years ago, I attended a weekend conference just outside Chilliwack, British Columbia, convened by Stó:lō Elders, scholars, and others wishing to present and discuss new cultural and historical findings. Apart from a few non-Indigenous anthropologists, there was one other non-Indigenous attendee, a man with red hair. On the final day we ended up at the lunch table together. He'd left his home in Scotland and retired to Chilliwack just over a year before, having chosen the town by looking at a map. I asked him why he'd decided to attend the conference. He'd been shocked, he said, by the disparaging way his non-Indigenous neighbours spoke about the Stó:lō whose land they unlawfully occupied. He was upset. He wanted to learn about Coast Salish cultures and history, and he wanted to meet Stó:lō people. "This sort of treatment is familiar to me," he said. "I served in a Scottish battalion during the Second World War and the British treated us the same way." Donald Harman Akenson recalls listening in as a British Army colonel, visiting the Royal Military College in Kingston, Ontario, compared the military units with which he'd served. "The Irish troops are best," he boasted. "Especially when headed by white officers." Donald Harman Akenson, *Surpassing Wonder: The Invention of the Bible and the Talmuds* (New York: Harcourt Brace & Company, 1998), 4.

5: *Six and a quarter inches from the pitch of its head ...* The subject of this poem is a Yup'ik wolf mask created in the late nineteenth century, possibly for a Kivgiq, or Messenger Feast, near Taciq (St. Michael), Alaska, on the coast of the Bering Sea. See Donald Ellis, Dawn Ades, Colin Browne, and Marie Mauzé, *Masks: Art of the Arctic; Reflections on the Unseen* (London, UK: Black Dog Publishing, 2015), 124 and 149. For other examples, see Ann Fienup-Riordan, *Agayuliyararput, Our Way of Making Prayer: The Living Tradition of Yup'ik Masks,* trans. Marie Meade, photography Barry McWayne (Seattle and London: University of Washington Press, in association with the Anchorage Museum of History and Art and the Anchorage Museum Association, 1996), 86, 119, and 236–237.

6: *to stop the Eskimo singing and dancing ...* The Aithúkāgûk, or "Inviting-In" Feast, to which Ernest William Hawkes was invited, occurred in the trading village of Taciq (St. Michael), Alaska, near the mouth of the Yukon River in January 1912. On the final day of the feast, the Uŋalaqłiq Chief addressed the U.S. military commander, who'd been invited so that the Chief might speak to him in public. The term "Eskimo," a remnant of settler culture, is on the wane in Alaska. Increasingly, Native Alaskans prefer to identify themselves by their cultural or tribal identity, such as Yup'ik or Iñupiat. I have retained "Eskimo" here to conform to the Chief's words as recorded in 1912 and mean no disrespect. See E.W. Hawkes, *The "Inviting-In" Feast of the Alaskan Eskimo,* Geological Survey Memoir 45, Anthropological Series no. 3 (Ottawa: Department of Mines, 1913), 3.

9: Yehuda ha-Levi was a Jewish theologian, physician, poet, and author of *The Kuzari*, or *The Book of Proof and Evidence in Support of the Abased Religion*. Influenced in part by Neoplatonism, *The Kuzari* argues that the faculty of reason places humans above all other species, and that prophecy is of a higher order than reason, revealing, with its "spiritual eye," divine intentions that logic and reason are incapable of recognizing.

13: The phrase *old bones ... among the rocks* is taken from an early draft of W.B. Yeats's final poem, "The Black Tower," written as Yeats was dying at Roquebrune-Cap-Martin in the south of France. The poem refers to the bones of ancient warriors but comes to mind when I reflect on the Great Hunger in Ireland (1845–1849). For an analysis of the different drafts of "The Black Tower," see Jon Stallworthy, *Between the Lines: W.B. Yeats's Poetry in the Making*, 2nd impression with corrections (Oxford, UK: Clarendon Press, 1965), 228.

13: *Indian meal.* Stuart John McLean, *The Event and Its Terrors: Ireland, Famine, Modernity*, Cultural Memory in the Present series (Palo Alto: Stanford University Press, 2004), 76.

13: *Naomi, Fanny, Agnes, Hannah, Maria, Marchioness of Abercorn, British Queen.* These are the names of "coffin ships" that transported Irish emigrants – unable to pay increased rents, cleared from their land, starving, and often stricken with typhus and dysentery – to Québec between 1846 and 1851. Hundreds died of illness aboard the ships or soon after their arrival in Canada. The journey itself was risky and dangerous. See Edward Laxton, *The Famine Ships: The Irish Exodus to America, 1846–51* (London, UK: Bloomsbury Publishing, 2016), 129–131.

15: *Gone West.* My old people used this expression when someone died, a euphemism derived from the classics, and a reference to the sinking sun at the end of the day, the solar journey being concluded.

17: *mowitch.* A Chinuk Wawa word for "deer." It was in common use when my grandfather, as a young man, homesteaded on the Goose Lake Road in 1912.

19: *Bialik's sprites:* tzafririm ... Haim Nahman Bialik, *Revealment and Concealment: Five Essays*, afterword Zali Gurevitch (Jerusalem: Ibis Editions, 2000), 120–124. The line is drawn from Bialik's youthful erotic poem "Sprites."

20: *Palestine has produced nothing but religions, sacred frenzies ...* Sigmund Freud, *Letters of Sigmund Freud*, trans. Tania and James Stern, ed. Ernst L. Freud (New York: Basic Books, 1975), 411–412. These lines occur in a letter to Arnold Zweig sent soon after Freud's seventy-sixth birthday in 1932.

20: *I can remember my father talking about one of their Sunday afternoon sports ...* Primrose Upton in David Mitchell and Dennis Duffy, eds., "Bright Sunshine and a Brand New Country: Recollections of the Okanagan Valley, 1890–1914," *Sound Heritage* 8, no. 3. (Victoria, BC: Ministry of Provincial Secretary and Government Services, Aural History Program, 1979): 50.

The Azure Notebook

25: *I fear to cut the pearl ...* Osip Mandelstam, "Ariosto," *Poems of Osip Mandelstam*, trans. Peter France (New York: New Directions, 2014), 53.

25: *four men around a table ...* Max Beckmann, *Four Men around a Table* (1943). When he made this painting, Beckmann was in hiding from the Nazis in Amsterdam.

31: *the year Blackshirts entered Rome ...* Mussolini's thugs marched into Rome in 1922.

31: *An' I thocht o' the last wild look ye gied / afore ye deed!* These lines are from "The Watergaw," the first poem by Scottish poet Hugh MacDiarmid to be published in the Doric, or Vernacular. "The Watergaw" appeared in *The Scottish Chapbook* in September 1922 under the name Hugh M'Diarmid. He offered up various spellings of his name in the early years: Hugh M'Diarmid, Hugh McDiarmid, Hugh Macdiarmid, and Hugh MacDiarmid. All were pseudonyms of Christopher Murray Grieve. See C.M. Grieve, "Introducing 'Hugh M'Diarmid,'" in Hugh MacDiarmid, *Selected Prose*, ed. Alan Riach (Manchester: Carcanet Press, 1992), 9.

32: *the inhuman.* Veit Erlmann, *Reason and Resonance: A History of Modern Aurality* (New York: Zone Books, 2010), 320.

32: *... since the war I have heard the radio for the first time ...* Gertrude

Stein and Thornton Wilder, *The Letters of Gertrude Stein and Thornton Wilder*, ed. Edward M. Burns and Ulla E. Dydo with William Rice (New Haven and London: Yale University Press, 1996), 245.

32: *the whole world a neighborhood* and *the extremely unfit.* Irving Fisher, quoted in Sylvia Nasar, *Grand Pursuit: The Story of Economic Genius* (New York: Simon and Schuster, 2011), 152 and 297–299. At the height of the eugenics hysteria in Europe and America in the early twentieth century, the U.S. established a highly restrictive immigration policy under the Immigration Act of 1924, or Johnson–Reed Act, which included the Asian Exclusion Act and the National Origins Act. The Act was established to prevent Asian immigration and to reduce all immigration by approximately 80 percent compared to pre-WWI levels. Applicants from Italy, Greece, Poland, Slavic nations and territories, and Jews, were refused. New funding was provided for tougher enforcement.

33: *with an authoritative government it would be easier to make the experiment of his economic system* and *the great forces that have no visible face.* Riccardo M. Degli Uberti, "Why Pound Liked Italy," in Sophokles, *Women of Trachis: A Version by Ezra Pound*, trans. Ezra Pound (New York: New Directions, 1957), 65.

33: *the guest of honour, Adolf Hitler.* Piers Brendon, *The Dark Valley: A Panorama of the 1930s* (New York: Knopf Doubleday, 2000), 567–568.

34: K'jipuktuk, in the Mi'kmaq language (Mi'kmawi'simk), is the name of the territory expropriated by British military personnel and settlers in order to build the garrison town of Halifax, Nova Scotia, in 1749.

36: *only months after Hinmatóowyalaht'qit, or Chief Joseph / approached the howitzer at C'aynnim ˀAlikinwaaspa …* Hinmatóowyalaht'qit, or Chief Joseph of the Niimíipuu (Nez Perce), surrendered to the U.S. Army at C'aynnim ˀAlikinwaaspa (Place of the Manure Fire), or Bear Paw Battlefield, in Montana Territory, on October 5, 1877. He and his people had tried to outrun the U.S. Army in an attempt to reach the Canadian border. Hinmatóowyalaht'qit placed his trust in the officers to whom he'd surrendered, hoping they'd keep their promise and allow his people to return home. The promise was broken. He struggled for years, without success, to defend his traditional territory against waves of settlers, and died in exile "on September 21, 1904, while he was sitting in front of his tipi fire. The Colville agency physician reported simply that he had died of a broken heart." Alvin M. Josephy, Jr., *The Nez Perce Indians and the Opening of the Northwest*, American Heritage Library (Boston and New York: Houghton Mifflin Company, 1997), 643.

36: *bright-eyed as hawks …* Walt Whitman, *Specimen Days and Collect*, intro. Leslie Jamison (Brooklyn and London: Melville House Publishing, 2014), 173.

36: Joseph Banks, naturalist, sailed on Cook's 1766 voyage to Newfoundland and was official scientist on Cook's first voyage to the South Seas aboard the *Endeavour* in 1767. He later became the head of the Royal Society.

37: *Our people who fish in those Parts …* Quoted in Nicholas Thomas, *Cook: The Extraordinary Voyages of Captain James Cook* (Toronto: Viking Canada, 2003), 7.

37: *That there was a woman in Gloucester, Massachusetts* and *an instance of the Pleistocene "boat" as such* are taken from the poem "LX VIII" printed on a single sheet of paper slipped into the inside front cover in Charles Olson's "*West*" (London, UK: Goliard Press, 1966).

37: *I've been absorbed by the subject of America all my life* is the first line of Charles Olson's paragraph-long introduction to "*West*."

38: *Das ist Karfreitagszauber, Herr!* In Richard Wagner, *Parsifal*, act 3 (1882). The final act of *Parsifal* takes place on Good Friday morning, a time of mystical renewal. Parsifal is unfamiliar with its sacred nature. The aged knight Gurnemanz tells him, "This is Good Friday's magic, sir!"

38: *Chagall's wounded bird* refers to a 1935 gouache by Marc Chagall, *The Bird Wounded by an Arrow*. The elegant bird, with its beautiful plumage, twists in painful agony; the bowman, like Wagner's Parsifal, appears to be surprised by the consequences of his act.

39: *a light pattern, fire-writing.* Walter Benjamin, *The Origin of German Tragic Drama*, trans. John Osborne, intro. George Steiner (London and New York: Verso, 2003), 213–214. Benjamin quotes Johann Wilhelm Ritter's description of sound patterns on a glass plate strewn with sand.

39: *I'd do it all again.* From an interview with my grandmother Nora Mackenzie (née Guernsey) in *Strathyre* (National Film Board, 1979, 25 min.). "Strathyre" was the name my grandfather Colin Mackenzie gave to the small ranch he built near Tk'emlúps (Kamloops) before the First World War.

39: *... the world is as he newly represents it. An immense flame.* Guillaume Apollinaire, *Apollinaire on Art: Essays and Reviews, 1902–1918*, trans. Susan Suleiman, ed. LeRoy C. Breunig, new foreword Roger Shattuck (Boston: MFA Publications, 2001), 280.

41: *Everyone is already tired.* Frantz Fanon, quoted in Adam Shatz, "Where Life Is Seized," review of *Écrits sur l'aliénation et la liberté* (2015), by Frantz Fanon, ed. Jean Khalfa and Robert Young, *London Review of Books* 39, no. 2 (January 2017): 19–27.

41: *ardour, cynicism, and violence.* Frantz Fanon, quoted in Frantz Fanon, *The Wretched of the Earth*, trans. Constance Farrington, preface Jean-Paul Sartre (London, UK: Penguin Books, 2001), 310.

41: *Every time we abandon an attitude of understanding ...* Frantz Fanon, quoted in Shatz, "Where Life Is Seized," 19–27.

42: *Daily life is set to the rhythm of a number of sounds ...* Frantz Fanon, quoted in Shatz, 19–27.

43: *by dray the stone was exhumed ...* The ancient standing stone, hauled, or dragged, and dug into the garden at Moniack Castle, is more properly called a menhir. It is known as the Stone of Balblair.

43: *Les parapluies de Cherbourg* (1964). Written and directed by Jacques Demy. Starring Catherine Deneuve and Nino Castelnuovo, this bittersweet love story, set during the Algerian War of Independence, is notable for its dialogue, which is sung throughout, and the remarkable colour palette deployed in every scene.

45: *I was bored to hell.* Francis Picabia, quoted in Mark Polizzotti, *Revolution of the Mind: The Life of André Breton* (New York: Farrar, Straus and Giroux, 1995), 119. Picabia's remark was first published in *Littérature*, n.s., 5 (October 1, 1922).

45: *Humanity lives in its fiction.* Blaise Cendrars, quoted in Michel Manoll, "Blaise Cendrars: The Art of Fiction," *The Paris Review* 37, no. 38 (Spring 1966). The interview was broadcast in France in the fall of 1950 and published two years later by Éditions Denoël as *Blaise Cendrars vous parle …*

46: *he explains that when the Royal Engineers …* The pronoun refers to poet Robert Graves. The air was absolutely still when the gas cocks were opened; it drifted back into the British trenches inflicting terrible casualties. Robert Graves, *Goodbye to All That*, rev. ed. (London, UK: Penguin Essentials, 2011 [1929]), 150–157 and 173–174.

46: *returned our loathing.* Graves, *Goodbye to All That*, 174.

46: *Dead Calm.* Graves, 157.

47: *Make of my head a prow …* Aimé Césaire, *Return to My Native Land*, trans. John Berger and Ana Bostock, intro. Mazisi Kunene (Harmondsworth: Penguin Books, 1969 [1939]), 77.

48: The *baptismal font* is Bedford Basin, a protected harbour adjacent to Halifax/K'jipuktuk. During the Second World War, it was the staging point for merchant convoys en route to Britain and the Soviet Union. As a naval officer in his early twenties, my father escorted supply ships across the North Atlantic from Bedford Basin. Their departure and arrival dates were kept secret to prevent enemy submarines from knowing the ships' positions.

48: *Mak ready, mak ready, my merry men aw!* The lines in italics are from the Scottish ballad "Sir Patrick Spens," a poem I memorized as a boy and which became attached to the ships that came and went in our lives in Nova Scotia. The King's order and the Captain's sense of duty overruled the sailor's prediction of a dire change in the weather: *A saw the new muin late yestreen / Wi the auld muin in her airm / And gif we gang tae sea, maister, / A fear we'll cam tae hairm.*

48: *Die Rote Fahne* (The Red Flag) was the revolutionary Spartacist newspaper established by Rosa Luxemburg and Karl Liebknecht in Berlin on November 9, 1918, the day after Luxemburg was released from prison.

49: *carrots of Empire.* The *Empresses* were fast passenger and freight ships built by the Canadian Pacific Railway to link China, Japan, and Hong Kong to Great Britain. On their arrival in Vancouver, passengers and freight, including silkworms, were transferred to waiting trains and transported across Canada at top speed. In Montréal, they were transferred to CPR ships for the final leg of the journey. At the turn of the twentieth century, domestic and foreign policies in the British Empire and its dominions were racially determined. It would not have surprised readers of Winston Churchill's *My African Journey* (1908) to be instructed that Canada's destiny was to become "a white man's country." Michael Makovsky, *Churchill's Promised Land: Zionism and Statecraft*, A New Republic Book (New Haven, CT: Yale University Press, 2007), 59.

50: *Françoise Gilot recalled the day in 1946 …* The account of Breton and Picasso meeting is taken from Françoise Gilot and Carlton Lake, *Life with Picasso* (New York: McGraw-Hill Book Company, 1964), 138–139. François Mauriac once described Breton as being "the exact opposite of Rimbaud. Until his last day on earth, he kept faith with the obstinate adolescent he had been." Wayne Andrews, *The Surrealist Parade* (Cambridge, MA: New Directions Publishing, 1990), 62.

50: *It's what I wanted and I've gotten it.* Gertrude Stein, quoted by Linda Wagner-Martin, *"Favoured Strangers": Gertrude Stein and Her Family* (New Brunswick, NJ: Rutgers University Press, 1995), 266.

51: *the foe of Éluard ...* André Breton. From his crates and packing boxes, Breton might have pulled out a copy of Edward Linnaeus Keithahn's *Monuments in Cedar: The Authentic Story of the Totem Pole* (Kichx̱áan [Ketchikan], AK: Roy Anderson), 1945.

52: *and you, Aragon?* Stalin had only recently died when the poet Louis Aragon – editor of the communist weekly *Les Lettres françaises* – asked Picasso to draw a sketch of young Stalin for the cover. It was a rush job, and Picasso's heart was not in it. Readers were furious with the result and took their anger out on Aragon. For an account of his humiliation, see Gilot and Lake, *Life with Picasso*, 256. His *mea culpa* can be found in Louis Aragon, "On a Portrait of Stalin," in Denis Hollier and Jeffrey Mehlman, eds, *Literary Debate: Texts and Contexts*, Postwar French Thought 2 (New York: The New Press, 1999), 82–87.

54: *on Roussel's syntactical Möbius strip.* Raymond Roussel, *Locus Solus*, Library of French Fiction (Philadelphia: D.N. Goodchild, 2007 [1914]), 1–5. Like Roussel's *Impressions of Africa* (1910), *Locus Solus* proceeds by means of homonymic puns.

56: *Père Le Jeune was building his New Jerusalem ...* Father Jean-Marie-Raphaël Le Jeune, or Père Le Jeune, was rector and superior of the Roman Catholic Diocese of Tk'emlúps (Kamloops) and presided over the Saint-Louis Mission on the bench across the Thompson River from the recently established city of Kamloops. He actively sought out new technologies to assist with his mission, including the adaptation of the Duployan shorthand method to inscribe Chinuk Wawa, also called Chinook Jargon, a polyglot language in use from Oregon to Alaska in the nineteenth and early twentieth centuries. For many years, Le Jeune published prayers, hymns, community notes, news, and advertisements using the shorthand alphabet in his periodical, the *Kamloops Wawa*, which was read by parishioners and much admired by missionaries around the world. In the shorthand alphabet, which he called *Chinuk pipa,* he was known as Papa Pir Lshyun.

57: *a poorly gotten up thing ...* This phrase is taken from a letter sent by Father Le Jeune on December 14, 1892, to a magazine called *The Stenographer.* One can see by his false modesty that he was, in fact, proud of his celebrated periodical, the *Kamloops Wawa*. The letter was published in the February 1893 issue of *The Stenographer*. David Douglas Robertson, "*Kamloops Wawa* in the *Stenographer* Magazine (Part 2)," December 10, 2019, chinookjargon.com/2019/12/10/kamloops-wawa-in-the-stenographer-magazine-part-2/#more-32523.

57: *Alta naika tomtom aias tlus naika iskom naika mashin, pi mamuk pipa kopa msaika mashin.* If you phonetically sound out and transcribe the first two lines of Father Le Jeune's first epistle to his parishioners, they would probably look something like this. The original text was written in a modified Duployan shorthand Le Jeune called *Chinuk pipa*. He used an Edison mimeograph to create multiple copies. The modest newsletter, a precursor to the *Kamloops Wawa*, was published on January 15, 1892. The translation is by David Douglas Robertson. See Robertson, "Le Jeune's First Letter to the Indigenous People," May 11, 2019, chinookjargon.com/2019/05/11/le-jeunes-first-letter-to-the-indigenous-people/.

57: *Louis Clexlixqen* (Xlexxle'xken, Klicktickkun, Tlihtlihen, Hatakun, Petit Louis), born in 1828, was a hereditary Secwépemc Chief, a position in which he served for sixty-three years. After converting to Roman Catholicism, he was appointed as a "Church Chief," a position established by the Oblates within their village council system. He raised money to build a church on the Tk'emlúpay Reserve and was an active supporter of day and residential schools for Secwépemc children. In 1866, Secwépemc Reserve lands were severely reduced by the provincial government. For the rest of his life, Louis worked to reclaim the territory seized by settlers from the Secwépemc, Nlaka'pamux, and Syilx people. Petit Louis died in 1915. Chief Johnny Chillihetza (Txelexitsa, Tselaxi'tsa), born in 1872 at Spaxomin, was a hereditary Chief, the grandson of Pelkamulox, and adopted son of Chief Nicola. He died in 1930.

57: *L'Européen le plus moderne ...* The phrase occurs in Apollinaire's 1912 poem "Zone," the initial poem in his 1913 collection, *Alcools*.

58: *wearing the antlers of his clan on his cap ...* My grandfather, Colin Mackenzie, applied for and received a commission in the Seaforth Highlanders in Vancouver, BC, in 1917, and was soon on his way to France.

60: *they'll come looking for us again one day.* Admiral Jackie Fisher, who in 1904 became First Sea Lord in Great Britain, believed that the Dominions should contribute to the cost of the Royal Navy's new dreadnoughts and heavy cruisers. Canadians countered that they had no enemies and were not interested in making a contribution. Fisher declared: "They are an unpatriotic, grasping people who only stick by us for the good they can get out of us." Margaret MacMillan, *The War That Ended Peace: The Road to 1914* (Toronto: Allen Lane, 2013), 124.

65: *Larraín's* Neruda. A ponderous 2016 biopic about Chilean poet Pablo Neruda, directed by Pablo Larraín.

65: *Birney's wartime English Bay ...* The reference is to poet Earle Birney, and to his poems "Vancouver Lights" (1941) and "Dusk on English Bay" (1941).

65: *i caught, in a glance, the eye of Allan King ...* Allan King was one of the world's great documentary filmmakers. His early films, *Skidrow* (1956), *Pemberton Valley* (1957), *Warrendale* (1967), and *A Married Couple* (1969) broke new ground. Later films, like *Dying at Grace* (2003), and *Memory for Max, Clair, Ida and Company* (2005), explored the solitary vigils that haunt every soul. He was courageous, intellectually curious, a great reader, deeply knowledgeable about music, and carried within him a healthy rage against institutional stupidity and authoritarianism in all their guises.

67: *asoqommtaqan.* "Bridge," according to Albert D. DeBlois's *Micmac Dictionary*, Mercury Series, Canadian Ethnology Service Paper 131 (Hull: Canadian Museum of Civilization, 1996), 7 and 10. The poem recalls the construction of the Angus L. MacDonald bridge in Halifax/K'jipuktuk in the mid-1950s. As children we were told that a "Micmac Chief" had lifted a curse on the bridge, allowing settlers to successfully complete the new span.

67: *Whipper Billy Watson*, Prince Maiava, his sideman and bongodrummer Coconut Willie, and the Kalmikoff brothers, Ivan and Karol, were wrestling sensations during the 1950s.

74: *INDIAN BOLOGNA, ACCORDING TO CURLY:* Curly has been a fisherman all his life. He and his brother made their own commercial fishing boats using a water-powered mill. He was born on the east coast of Vancouver Island on Sansum Narrows. This is an old recipe but a good one, especially when living aboard a boat.

Vancouver in Translation

The poems by Guillaume Apollinaire, Blaise Cendrars, and Marcel Thiry included here were originally published in *The Capilano Review*, 3.23 (Spring 2014), along with a conversation between Ian Wallace and myself which began with our musing about the mention of Vancouver by French poets in the early years of the twentieth century. I would like to thank Michèle Smolkin for assistance with the translations. My thanks also to editor Jenny Penberthy for her generosity and to Ian Wallace for his friendship and for our ongoing, stimulating conversations.

79: *Hollow trees that hug vagabond* Câpresses / Chabins *sing songs to die for / to their chestnut-haired* Chabines. Apollinaire in these three lines refers to residents of the French Antilles, a French colony in the Caribbean that included the islands of Gwadloup and Matinik. In the racialized language of the time (1912), *Câpresse* was the term for a woman with one-quarter Black ancestry, which is to say that she had one Black grandparent. *Chabin* and *Chabine* are Kwéyòl words for men and women with one Black great-grandparent. The word *Chabine* often referred to a light-skinned woman of African descent with red-brown, gold, or blonde hair. Apollinaire's lines are "*Les Chabins chantent des airs à mourir / Aux Chabines marronnes.*" The adjective *marronnes* also refers to slaves who have escaped from their masters and live in freedom. I'm sure that Apollinaire liked blending both meanings. In an earlier translation, I wrote: "To fugitive Chabines."

80: *And the wa wa goose trumpets in the north …* Gérald Purnelle, in his edition of Apollinaire's *Calligrammes* (Paris: GF Flammarion, 2018), notes that "*wawa* or *wewe* is the Indian name for the wild goose in Canada. The passage in lines 24–29 of 'Les fenêtres' is inspired by the novel *La Quarteronne* by Thomas Mayne Reid where, according to Apollinaire's notes, he discovered this 'wa wa goose'" (200). Reid's novel *The Quadroon* was published in 1856. Ron Padgett notes that in later versions of the poem, Apollinaire alters the cry to "oua oua," and "oua-oua." Guillaume

Apollinaire, *Zone: Selected Poems*, trans. Ron Padgett, NYRB Poets Series (New York Review Books, 2015), 244.

82: *You who grow pale at the mention of Vancouver* ("Toi qui pâlis au nom de Vancouver"). The version of Thiry's poem translated here is taken from Pierre Seghers, ed., *Le livre d'or de la poésie française des origines à 1940*, intro. Pierre Seghers, Collection Marabout université (Vervier, Belgium: Nouvelles Éditions Marabout), 1972.

Traveller

86: *Donald Brittain's* Memorandum ... Directed by Donald Brittain, filmed and edited by John Spotton, *Memorandum* (National Film Board of Canada, 1966) remains one of the most powerful and insightful documentary films to address the Shoah. In the wake of Hannah Arendt's 1963 account of the Adolf Eichmann trial, *Eichmann in Jerusalem: A Report on the Banality of Evil*, Brittain and Spotton travelled to Poland and Germany to ask if the roots of authoritarianism, state violence, and intolerance do not remain close to the surface in European culture.

88: *galaga snaanga*. This is one of the names in X̱aad Kíl – the Massett dialect of Haida – for a figure commonly known in English as Fungus or Fungus Man. In one of the Haida Oral Histories, Raven is asked by his wife and sister to collect vaginas from a reef in X̱aayda gwaay so that they may bear children and enjoy relations with men. He enlists several helpers as steersmen, all of whom fail to steady the canoe as it approaches the reef. Fungus Man saves the day! See Colin Browne, *Entering Time: The Fungus Man Platters of Charles Edenshaw* (Vancouver, BC: Talonbooks, 2016).

89: Rockingham is a suburb of Halifax/K'jipuktuk.

92: *I forgot the amount you gave me for the box ...* Henry Edenshaw to C.F. Newcombe, April 2, 1906. Henry Edenshaw, or Edensaw – *Gwyaawhlans* (*Kihlguulins*) in X̱aad Kíl – was a cousin of the artist Da.a xiigang (Charles Edenshaw) and a resident of the village of Massett. He was a lay preacher in the Anglican Church and a translator of religious texts, including chapters of the *Holy Bible*, into Haida. He assisted Charles Newcombe by helping to acquire and identify Haida cultural belongings destined, in 1906, for the Field Museum in Chicago.

92: *it was the year Emily Carr met Sewiṉchelwet in Vancouver ...* Sewiṉchelwet is the Sḵwx̱wú7mesh name given to Emily Carr's friend Sophie Frank (1872–1939) when she was born. After her marriage to Jimmy Frank, Sophie moved to Eslhá7an, or Mission Reserve No. 1, in what is now North Vancouver. The two women first met in Vancouver in 1906 when Sophie, having paddled over to the city to sell her baskets, knocked on the door of Emily Carr's studio.

92: *A page of "A Little Cloud" ...* James Joyce, quoted in Richard Ellman, *James Joyce*, rev. ed. (Oxford: Oxford University Press, 1982), 232.

94: *Do you not know that in real death ...* Michel de Montaigne, *The Essays: A Selection*, trans. Michael Andrew Screech (London, UK: Penguin Books, 2004), 33. These lines are attributed to the Roman poet Lucretius and appear in Montaigne's essay "That to Philosophize Is to Learn How to Die."

94: *Marjerie and Malcolm ...* During the 1940s, the novelists Margerie and Malcolm Lowry lived for several years in a fisherman-built squatter's shack at Dollarton on Burrard Inlet near Vancouver where Malcolm Lowry wrote the novel *Under the Volcano* (New York: Reynal & Hitchcock, 1947).

96: *The following is a list of his favourite colours ...* Duncan Campbell Scott, *Walter J. Phillips*, Canadian Art series (Toronto: Ryerson Press, 1947), 24.

Seventy-Four Prepositions

97: *the Battle of Jutland ...* As a Wolf Cub I was riveted by Baden Powell's account of Jack Cornwell, a sixteen-year-old Boy (1st Class) in the Royal Navy who remained at his station during the Battle of Jutland in 1916, although the gun crew he'd been assisting had been decimated by German shells. Cornwell died of his wounds and was posthumously awarded the Victoria Cross.

99: *Playa Bonita*. A beach northwest of Puerto Limón in Costa Rica.

100: *colombiano*, or "Colombian wrench." After several days on the wharves in Colón, Panama, seeking passage to Colombia, I met the captain of a cabin cruiser who, in return for my offer of help, agreed to take me to the island of San Andrés, twenty-four hours to the north. When we were at last cleared to leave the harbour, having accepted two more backpackers and a fellow who may have committed a crime – the government wanted him out of the country – the sky was clear. By midnight we were being tossed about by a powerful storm and taking on water. The backpackers started bailing. The young man shinnied up to the top of the short mast. The boat was not well maintained. It soon became clear that we'd have to replace the head gasket on the engine. With the hull shuddering at every plunge, Corjo, the skipper, dug around on the bridge and produced a hammer and a large screwdriver. He grinned at me. "*El colombiano*," he shouted over the wind, "the Colombian wrench," and proceeded to tap the heads of the hexagonal bolts until each of them moved and we could turn them by hand. An hour or two later the gas line broke and we began to drift in the darkness. We could hear breakers on the shore. The owner of the boat sent a man out to look for us when we lost radio contact and failed to arrive on time. He found us sometime after dawn, and after many attempts to rig up a line, managed to tow us into port where everyone quickly disappeared.

100: Walt Kelly was the revered creator of *Pogo*. I sat with him briefly at the bar one evening at a conference in Montréal, where I also had the honour of meeting the journalist Bernard Fall who had witnessed the Battle of Điện Biên Phủ. Fall was tragically killed in Vietnam a few months later, in February 1967.

101: *La Bonza Unchained*. A witty musical performed at the McPherson Playhouse in Victoria during the 1970s. It took pointed aim at the provincial Social Credit government of the day, and particularly Premier Bill Bennett, who sings "Everything's Mine!"

107: *SALT SPRING:* This poem is dedicated to the memory of Marjorie and Bevill Acland, and their dog Taffy, whose faces always seem in my memory to be bathed in western light.

109: *Canada's contribution to the twentieth century ...* This passage refers to the industrial and residential school system established by the Dominion government and the nation's churches to erase Indigenous languages and cultures. The school alluded to is the Kuper Island Indian Residential School (1899–1975), a deadly source of infection and a place of intolerable mental and physical suffering. It has since been demolished. Kuper Island has been renamed Penelakut Island.

Improvisations 1–12

111: *It may even be true that the predicaments of our time ...* Arendt's "Ideology and Terror: A Novel Form of Government," appeared in the *Review of Politics* 15, no. 3 (July 1953): 303. The essay was added to later editions of Arendt's *The Origins of Totalitarianism*, first published in 1951.

113: *Historical knowledge, at least in the modern west ...* McLean, *The Event and Its Terrors*, 17.

113: *It has no sexual guideposts ...* Dorothy Jean Ray, *A Legacy of Arctic Art*, foreword Aldona Jonaitis, photography Barry McWayne (Vancouver, BC: Douglas & McIntyre, 1996), 84.

113: Siqnazuaq is the Iñupiat name for the town of Nome in what is now called Alaska.

114: Ugiuvak is also known as King Island Village, Alaska.

114: *used to drill a hole ...* Dorothy Jean Ray, *Artists of the Tundra and the Sea* (Seattle and London: University of Washington Press, 1980), 151.

116: *to discover or perceive properties of the object which are normally concealed ...* Claude Lévi-Strauss, interviewed by Georges Charbonnier, in *Conversations with Claude Lévi-Strauss,* trans. John and Doreen Weightman, ed. Georges Charbonnier (London, UK: Jonathan Cape, 1970), 125.

118: *Essais de reconstitution d'objets ...* Christian Boltanski's moving "memory works" were created in 1970–1971. Several were included in the travelling *Christian Boltanski: Lessons of Darkness* exhibition in 1989.

119: *The Sympseyan Indians arrived with potatoes for sale ...* and the two following quotes can be found in the "Journal of the Hudson's Bay Company at Fort Simpson, 1834–1837" (manuscript), Bancroft Collection, vol. 4. See also Marius Barbeau, *Totem Poles of the Gitksan, Upper Skeena River, British Columbia*, Bulletin no. 61, Anthropological Series no. 12 (Ottawa: Department of Mines, National Museum of Canada, and, F.A. Acland, Printer to the King's Most Excellent Majesty, 1929), 206.

119: *A year later, Haidas sold the occupiers eight hundred bushels.* Richard Somerset Mackie, *Trading Beyond the Mountains: The British Fur Trade on the Pacific, 1793–1843* (Vancouver, BC: UBC Press, 1997), 291–292.

119: *I had in my cellar, he wrote, a firkin of potatoes ...* Henry David Thoreau, *Walden, or Life in the Woods, and "Civil Disobedience,"* intro. W.S. Merwin, afterword William Howarth (New York: Signet Classics, 2012 [1849 and 1854]), 198.

119: *arrowheads.* Michael Sims, *The Adventures of Henry Thoreau: A Young Man's Unlikely Path to Walden Pond* (London, UK: Bloomsbury, 2014), 280–281.

119: *Unangax̂.* This term replaces *Aleut*, a term introduced by Russian "explorers" and traders when they first encountered the people living in Tanam Unangaa (the Aleutian Islands).

119: *Before I arrived 30,000 male seals had been killed in a single day.* Owen Matthews, *Glorious Misadventures: Nikolai Rezanov and the Dream of a Russian America* (New York: Bloomsbury Publishing USA, 2013), 207–209. The penises were air-dried, shipped to China, and sold as an aphrodisiac.

119: *both Tsar and God.* Matthews, *Glorious Misadventures*, 211.

121: *Unión Revolucionaria de las Juventudes Ecuatorianas* (Revolutionary Union of Ecuador Youth). Régis Debray, *Strategy for Revolution*, trans. Rosemary Sheed, ed. Robin Blackburn (Harmondsworth: Pelican Books, 1973), 41.

122: *Revolution is water gushing out of the ground.* Debray, *Strategy for Revolution*, 124.

123: Blenny information is courtesy of W.A. Clemens and G.V. Wilby, *Fishes of the Pacific Coast of Canada*, Bulletin no. LXVIII, rev. ed. (Ottawa: Fisheries Research Board of Canada, 1949).

123: Gwa'yi, or Tsawataineuk, the home of the Dzawada'enuxw of the Kwakwa̱ka̱'wakw First Nation, is, in English, called Kingcome. The Gwa'yi River, fed by a melting glacier, flows into Kingcome Inlet, where the three-foot-long wrymouth blenny was caught. See First Nations Land Rights and Environmentalism in British Columbia, "Kwakwa̱ka̱'wakw," March 5, 2020, www.firstnations.eu/fisheries/kwakwakawakw.htm.

124: *the enemy rose out of the sea.* On June 20, 1942, the lighthouse and the RDF (radio direction finder) installation at Estevan Point on Vancouver Island's west coast were shelled by Japanese submarine *I-26*. Its deck gun, operated by chief gunner Hashiro Hayashi, fired twenty-five to thirty rounds from two miles out, all of which missed their targets. *I-26* was stationed off the Strait of Juan de Fuca before the attack on Pearl Harbor on December 7, 1941, one of several submarines sent to attack shipping and land installations on the Pacific Coast. U.S. and Canadian authorities actively suppressed information about their presence and their activities.

125: *for around [Him] a cloud has been fixed.* From the *Pseudo-Orphica* (Recension B), as it appears in Clement of Alexandria's *Stromata* (*Miscellanies*), 124. Cited in James L. Kugel, *The Bible as It Was* (Cambridge, MA: Belknap Press of Harvard University Press, 1997), 139 and 600–601.

126: *A quick glance at the* Liebesnacht *was all he needed to lay down his pen.* Puccini despaired that he'd ever write a love duet to equal Wagner's *Liebesnacht* for *Tristan and Isolde*. According to Peter Conrad: "At the end of his life, struggling to conclude *Turandot* with a love duet that might stand beside that in *Tristan*, Puccini acknowledged the fatality of this influence. He sneaked a look at Wagner's score, and soon wished he had not. 'Enough of this music!' he wrote. 'This tremendous music destroys one and renders one incapable of composing anymore.'" Peter Conrad,

Verdi and/or Wagner: Two Men, Two Worlds, Two Centuries (London, UK: Thames and Hudson, 2011), 263.

126: *una suprema verità d'amore ...* From the published score of Giacomo Puccini's 1910 opera *La fanciulla del West* (*The Girl of the Golden West*), an opera in three acts (based on the drama by David Belasco), 330–332. The English translation in the 1910 original libretto reads: "... the best and highest teaching of love, [my brothers,] that the very worst of sinners may be redeemed and shall find the way to Paradise!"

126: *our good-for-nothing Italians, this mediocre race.* Benito Mussolini's reforestation scheme for the Apennines is mentioned in Brendon, *The Dark Valley*, 567–568.

127: *Auguste Salzmann's calotype ...* James S. Ackerman, *Origins, Imitation, Conventions: Representation in the Visual Arts* (Cambridge, MA: MIT Press, 2002), 110.

127: *The original condition of the earth was quite different ...* Jean-Jacques Rousseau, quoted in Paolo Rossi, *The Dark Abyss of Time: The History of the Earth and the History of Nations from Hooke to Vico*, trans. Lydia G. Cochrane (Chicago and London: University of Chicago Press, 1987), 264.

127: Da.a xiigang is one of the names of Haida artist Charles Edenshaw or Edensaw.

127: *Stones are generated as plants are ...* Johannes Christophorus Schweigger, *De ortu lapidum* (1665), quoted in Rossi, *The Dark Abyss of Time*, 7.

128: *hayash-tayi.* For more information on Powell's first inspection tour as Superintendent, see Israel Wood Powell, *Report of the Superintendent for Indian Affairs for British Columbia for 1872 & 1873* (Ottawa: I.B. Taylor, 1873). Available online at dx.doi.org/10.14288/1.0221711. On June 13, 1874, the *Cariboo Sentinel* published a brief item on Powell's much anticipated visit to Tk'emlúps (Kamloops) in which he is called *hyas tyhee* (Great Chief). David Douglas Robertson, "What Do You Call an Indian Commissioner in Jargon?," December 28, 2019, chinookjargon.com/2019/12/28/1874-bc-what-do-you-call-an-indian-commissioner-in-jargon/.

128: *supposedly murdered the crew of the* George S. Wright. Alan Thomas, "Photography of the Indian: Concept and Practice on the Northwest Coast," *BC Studies* 52 (Winter 1981–1982): 74–76.

128: *Mexican and Spanish improvers …* John Frazier Henry, *Early Maritime Artists of the Pacific Northwest Coast, 1741–1841* (Vancouver and Toronto: Douglas & McIntyre, 1984), 106–107.

129: Midshipman Henry Humphrys, "Port Dick, near Cook's Inlet" (1794). See James K. Barnett, "The End of the Northern Mystery: George Vancouver's Survey of the Northwest Coast," in James K. Barnett and David L. Nicandri, eds., *Arctic Ambitions: Captain Cook and the Northwest Passage* (Anchorage: Anchorage Museum, Cook Inlet Historical Society, and the Washington State History Museum in association with the University of Washington Press, 2015), 274 and 278–280.

129: *panspermic.* In an excerpt from *Mundus subterraneus* (1644), quoted by Paolo Rossi, Athanasius Kircher observes that "The *panspermia* or *vis seminalis* that produced physical reality was a material spirit 'composed both of more subtle celestial air and of portions of the elements.' It was a 'spiritous sulfureo-salino-mercurial vapor' that was 'the universal seed of things created with the elements, and the origin of all of the things in the world.'" Rossi, *The Dark Abyss of Time,* 8.

129: *old nations … mothers of civility.* Riccardo M. Degli Uberti, "Why Pound Liked Italy," 64.

129: E.J. Hughes was a distinguished Canadian war artist and committed contemporary artist, one of the nation's most recognizable landscape and seascape artists of the twentieth century. His postwar paintings of local ferry boats in British Columbia waters quickly became iconic.

129: *The instinct of the nation will never be content without a share in the booty which it sees its neighbours greedily dividing.* Lord Salisbury, quoted in MacMillan, *The War That Ended Peace*, 38.

130: *As the country becomes impoverished the Company reduce their outfits ...* These lines are taken from John McLean, *Notes of a Twenty-Five Years' Service in the Hudson's-Bay Territory*, vol. 2 (London, UK: Richard Bentley, 1849), 266–299. They were reprinted in the appendices of a pamphlet published by the Aborigines' Protection Society entitled *Canada West and the Hudson's-Bay Company: A Political and Humane Question of Vital Importance to the Honour of Great Britain, to the Prosperity of Canada, and to the Existence of the Native Tribes; Being an Address to the Right Honourable Henry Labouchere, Her Majesty's Principal Secretary of State for the Colonies* (London, UK: William Tweedie, 1856), 18. Members of the Aborigines' Protection Society lobbied the British Colonial Office throughout the nineteenth century to recognize Indigenous Rights across Western Canada.

131: *That's a nice snake I've reared in my bosom.* Kaiser Wilhelm II, quoted in MacMillan, *The War That Ended Peace*, 65–66.

131–133: *Ten years on, the Geological Survey of Canada ...* The geological descriptions are taken from H.S. Bostock, *A Catalogue of Selected Airphotographs*, Geological Survey of Canada Paper 67, no. 48 (Ottawa: Department of Energy, Mines and Resources, 1968), 75, 24, 119, 23, 140, and 146.

134: *Here is my beloved son.* Serge Gruzinski, *The Aztecs: Rise and Fall of an Empire*, trans. Paul G. Bahn (London, UK: Thames and Hudson, 1992), 40.

134: *sadness and solitude* and *pleasure and contentment*, quoted in Fernando Cervantes, *The Devil in the New World: The Impact of Diabolism in New Spain* (New Haven and London: Yale University Press, 1994), 44.

134: *where God hath a temple, the devil will have a chapel ...* Robert Burton, *The Anatomy of Melancholy*, 2nd partition, ed. Holbrook Jackson (New York Review Books, 2001 [1621]), 321.

134: "*the melancholy juice.*" Burton, *The Anatomy of Melancholy*, 1st partition, 413.

134: *What makes them so freely venture their lives ...* Burton, *The Anatomy of Melancholy*, 2nd partition, 335.

135: *the Tzitzimitl is skeletal with raptor's talons and bird's eyes for joints ...* The description of Tzitzimitl is drawn from an image in Cervantes, *The Devil in the New World*, 44–45.

135: *the greatest monarch in Christendom.* Niccolò Machiavelli's assessment of King Ferdinand. Mark Cocker, *Rivers of Blood, Rivers of Gold: Europe's Conquest of Indigenous Peoples* (New York: Grove Press, 1998), 76.

135: *like Orinocos of the human heart.* Charles Baudelaire, *The Painter of Modern Life and Other Essays,* trans. and ed. Jonathan Mayne (London, UK: Phaidon, 1995), 24.

135: *The Gramscis and the Terracinis know they are almost nothing at this time ...* Victor Serge, *Notebooks, 1936–1947*, trans. Mitchell Abidor and Richard Greeman, ed. Claudio Albertani and Claude Rioux (New York Review Books, 2019), 290. Antonio Gramsci and Umberto Terracini were members of the Italian Communist Party and founders and editors of the weekly newspaper *L'Ordine Nuovo.* Gramsci was elected to the Italian parliament as a deputy in 1924. Terracini later edited the communist paper *L'Unita.* Both had been in prison for several years by 1931 when Serge wrote these words in *Literature and Revolution* (1932).

136: *LETTRE DE PARIS:* An earlier version of this poem was read at the Vancouver Art Gallery in July 2018 in the galleries of its summer exhibitions: *Cabin Fever* and *David Milne: Modern Painting.* Many thanks to Stephanie Bokenfohr and cheyanne turions for the invitation, and to my fellow poets who were part of this project.

136: *At night the furs of Sacher-Masoch become phosphorescent ...* Salvador Dalí, quoted in Andrews, *The Surrealist Parade*, 96.

136: *He had no ear for music ...* According to Buñuel, Breton "detested music, especially the opera." Luis Buñuel, *My Last Sigh*, trans. Abigail Israel (New York: Vintage Books, 1984), 113.

136: *The field mouse, on the other hand, was enthralled by Thoreau's debut on the flute ...* Sims, *The Adventures of Henry Thoreau*, 257–258.

136: *I have often thought of Gabriel the archangel ...* Antonin Artaud, quoted in Andrews, 129.

137: *That government is best which governs least.* Thoreau, "Civil Disobedience," in *Walden, or Life in the Woods and "Civil Disobedience,"* 275.

139: *At the century's end, Chief Johnny Muldoe found thirty-five stone clubs ...* The thirty-five stone clubs discovered by Chief Johnny Muldoe in 1898 are believed to be two to three thousand years old. Knut R. Fladmark, *British Columbia Prehistory* (Ottawa: Archeological Survey of Canada, National Museum of Man, and National Museums of Canada, 1986), 70–71.

139: *In those days, Queen Vic ruled rock forms on the White Lake Road.* The rock formation known as Queen Vic faces White Lake Ranch near snpintktn (Penticton), British Columbia. White Lake itself is little more than an alkali pond, and although it dries into a white disk during the heat of summer, it offers food and refreshment to sandhill cranes migrating over the valley each year.

139–140: *The pole, K'ëgit, was raised at dusk outside the Musée de l'Homme in January 1939.* The artist Kurt Seligmann shared an appreciation for Northwest Coast monumental and ceremonial art with his surrealist colleagues André Breton and Wolfgang Paalen. In 1938, he and his wife Arlette Paraf spent the summer in Hazelton, British Columbia. The pole purchased by Seligmann, with pressure applied by the local Indian Agent, was taken from the village of Tse-Kya in Hagwilget Canyon. It stands today in the foyer of the Musée du quai Branly in Paris. See Mélanie H. Morin in coll. with the Wet'suwit'en First Nation and the School District No. 54 (Bulkley Valley, BC), *Niwhts'ide'nï Hibi'it'ën, the Ways of Our Ancestors: Witsuwit'en History and Culture throughout the Millennia* (Smithers, BC: School District No. 54 [Bulkley Valley], 2011), 77.

140: *In the narrow canyon, Seligmann had admired its patina.* Le mat Keïgiet, *he wrote*, a une belle patine qui varie du gris argent au brun cuivré.

A translation would read: "The pole, Keïgiet, has a beautiful patina, varying from silver grey to a coppery brown." Kurt Seligmann, "Le mât-totem de Gédem Skanísh (Gyaedem Skanees)," *Journal de la Société des américanistes* 31 (1939): 126, doi.org/10.3406/jsa.1939.1985.

140: Christian Boltanski's assessment of the Musée de l'Homme is taken from Marjorie Perloff, "'What Has Occurred Only Once': Barthes' Winter Garden / Boltanski's Archives of the Dead," in Jean-Michel Rabaté, ed., *Writing the Image after Roland Barthes*, New Cultural Studies series (Philadelphia: University of Pennsylvania Press, 1997), 43.

140: *The train from Barcelona will soon arrive at Gare d'Austerlitz* ... In early 1939, approximately five hundred thousand Spanish refugees crossed the border into France looking for a safe haven. They were apprehended by French police. Men were marched off to concentration camps. Most felt they were being treated as criminals. Brendon, *The Dark Valley*, 600.

140: *Long live Death!* Edmundson, *The Death of Sigmund Freud: The Legacy of His Last Days* (New York: Bloomsbury, 2007), 221.

140: *saisissant.* This adjective appeared in the journal *Mundo Latino* (April/May 1939). Yannick Meunier, "Keïgiet, le géant au cœur palmaire," *Société suisse des Américanistes / Schweizerische Amerikanisten-Gesellschaft* 69 (2005): 80.

140: *When I search for Man in the technique and the style of Europe* ... Fanon, *The Wretched of the Earth*, 252.

140: *the rendezvous point for a lot of the soldiers*, quoted in Morin, *Niwhts'ide'nï Hibi'it'ën*, 310–312.

141: *Palais de Chaillot.* The home of the Musée de l'Homme in the 16th arrondissement of Paris.

141: *honorary SS officer Hanns Johst.* Johst was the author of the often-adapted quip, "When I hear the word culture ... I take the safety catch off my Browning," which appeared in the first act of his 1933 play *Schlageter*, a dramatic tribute to a Nazi martyr. Niall Ferguson, *The War of the World: Twentieth-Century Conflict and the Descent of the West* (New York: Penguin Press, 2006), 402.

141: *Thith-hak-key.* "In the Drawers," *MOA Magazine* 5 (Summer 2018): 17, UBC Museum of Anthropology (Vancouver, BC).

143: *Iralum Yua*, Spirit of the Moon-Woman. See Dorothy Jean Ray, *Eskimo Masks: Art and Ceremony*, photographs Alfred A. Blaker (Seattle and London: University of Washington Press, 1975), front cover, opposite p. 23, and 172–174; and Chuna McIntyre with Sean Mooney, "Masks in Detail," in Sean Mooney and Chuna McIntyre, eds., *Yua: Henri Matisse and the Inner Arctic Spirit*, with contributions by Patrice Deparpe, Ira Jacknis, Marie Mauzé, and Diana F. Pardue (Phoenix, AZ: Heard Museum, 2018), 106–107.

143: *I dreamed last night, I said, of* Trois têtes. À l'amitié ... These drawings by Henri Matisse were made *circa* 1951–1952 in consultation with André Rouveyre in memory of their mutual friend Guillaume Apollinaire, who died in 1918 of the Spanish Flu and his war wounds. See Patrice Deparpe, "Henri Matisse and His Eskimo Portraits," in McIntyre with Mooney, *Yua: Henri Matisse and the Inner Arctic Spirit*, 54–55.

143: *who can forget his plea ... ?* On the day he died from the Spanish flu on November 9, 1918, a doctor came to visit Apollinaire. The ailing poet is said to have cried out, "Save me, doctor! I want to live! I still have so many things to say!" These words were recalled by his widow, Jacqueline, the morning after he died. Francis Steegmuller, *Apollinaire: Poet Among the Painters* (Harmondsworth: Penguin Books, 1973), 272 and 314.

144: *Among the accessions by the Smithsonian Institution ...* See the *Annual Report of the Board of Regents of the Smithsonian Institution, Showing the Operations, Expenditures, and Condition of the Institution for the Year Ending June 30* (Washington, DC: Government Printing Office, 1906), 55, 57, 63, 75, 77, and 94.

144: *as a factor in revolution ...* Wolfgang Paalen, quoted in Serge, *Notebooks 1937–1947*, 216.

145: *there were always the portraits of men who had been hanged.* Richard Greeman, "Introduction" to Victor Serge, *Men in Prison*, trans. Richard Greeman (London, UK: Writers and Readers Publishing Cooperative, 1977), x.

145: *This war teaches us to be certain of our hates ...* Gertrude Stein, "All Sunday," in *Alphabets and Birthdays* (New Haven: Yale University Press, 1957), 113. Stein wrote "All Sunday" in Mallorca during the summer of 1915, the year my grandfather's brother Kenneth Mackenzie was killed in France.

145: *two "prehistoric" fossil ivory figures said to be from Norton Sound.* See Wolfgang Paalen, "About the Origins of the Doric Column and the Guitar-Woman," *DYN* 2 (July–August 1942): 16, in Christian Kloyber, ed., *Wolfgang Paalen's* DYN, *The Complete Reprint* (Vienna and New York: Springer Verlag, 2000).

145: *And those who hopped, or leapt, or grabbed a hand ...* The harrowing act of leaping onto an iceberg from a sinking ship is recounted in Laxton, *The Famine Ships*, 124–133.

145: *the peace of God, which passeth all understanding ...* This phrase is drawn from Paul's letters to the Philippians 4:7. Every Sunday it concluded the Anglican services I attended as a boy. The full blessing reads: "And the peace of God, which passeth all understanding, shall keep your hearts and minds through Christ Jesus."

Petal

On May 4, 2018, at the Vancouver East Cultural Centre, composer Alfredo Santa Ana and I presented an evening of new music and text we called *Music for a Night in May. Petal* was written in collaboration with Alfredo and became the final piece on the program, which included two other compositions: *Night Sonnets* and *Entr'Acte. Petal* began as a short poem. At first, we imagined a single song, but, as the collaboration advanced, we realized that we had unconsciously been working with a three-act narrative structure. By the time of its premiere eighteen months later, *Petal* had become a 38-minute composition for string quartet, soprano, and voice. Our soprano that evening was the brilliant Carla Huhtanen. The members of the string quartet – Nicholas Wright, Karen Gerbrecht, Andrew Brown, and Olivia Blander, all from the Vancouver Symphony – were superb, and they inspired all of us. Our wonderful conductor was Vern Griffiths, the VSO's principal percussionist. We were blessed to have been able to work with these extraordinary artists. For more, please see the chapbook issued on the evening of the performance, also entitled *Music for a Night in May.*

150: *the best jobs round here are plating the APCs ... the best jobs round here are plating the APCs ...* The abbreviation APC refers to an Armoured Personnel Carrier.

Envoi

161: *on the curtains and frosted windows in Kagurazaka ...* Kagurazaka (神楽坂) is a neighbourhood in Tokyo, northwest of Iidabashi Station.

+

"In His Fine Hand" appeared in an earlier version in *Supplement V.2*, published with the support of the Creative Writing Program and Kelly Writer's House at the Center for Programs in Contemporary Writing at the University of Pennsylvania, and in collaboration with Materialist Press, 2018. My grateful thanks go to the editors, Ariel Resnikoff and Orchid Tierney.

The three poems that appear in translation in the section entitled "Vancouver in Translation" were first published in *The Capilano Review*, 3.23 (Spring 2014), in a section entitled "Vancouver in Translation: A Conversation with Ian Wallace." Grateful thanks to the editor, Jenny Penberthy. The translations have been slightly revised since their initial publication.

Acknowledgments

I am grateful for the companionship of those who contributed to this book directly or indirectly, knowingly or unknowingly, who listened, who guided me, who worked with me, who opened my eyes and ears, who sustained me thereby. My heartfelt thanks to Sonny Assu, Daina Augaitis, Hugh Brody, Susan Browne, Neil Campbell, Barbara Cranmer, *Goothl Ts'imilx* Mike Dangeli, *Sm Łoodm 'Nüüsm* Mique'l Dangeli, Christos Dikeakos, Karen Duffek, Perry Eaton, Donald Ellis, Aaron Glass, Bruce Grenfell, Alan Hoover, Katia Kukawka, Daphne Marlatt, Marie Mauzé, Eric Metcalfe, Mélanie Morin, Andreas Neufert, David Pay, Gerald Peary, Jenny Penberthy, Judith Penner, Meredith Quartermain, Peter Quartermain, Colin Ritchie, Renee Rodin, Alfredo Santa Ana, Charles Simard, Les Smith, Michèle Smolkin, Karl Spreitz, Juliet Stevenson, Fenn Stewart, Catriona Strang, Charlotte Townsend-Gault, Seán Virgo, Fred Wah, Ian Wallace, John Walker, Anna Wang, *Gid7ahl-G̱udsllaay Lalaxaaygans* Terri-Lynn Williams-Davidson, Kevin Williams, Carol Yaple …

… and especially to Marian Penner Bancroft and Susanna Browne, the joys of my life, who don't let me get away with anything.

COLIN BROWNE has published five volumes of poetry. His most recent publications are *Entering Time: The Fungus Man Platters of Charles Edenshaw* (Talonbooks, 2016) and *The Hatch: Poems and Conversations* (Talonbooks, 2015). His books have been nominated for a Governor General's Literary Award and the Dorothy Livesay Award Poetry Prize. He is a celebrated filmmaker; his experimental documentary *White Lake* was nominated for a Genie Award for Best Feature Documentary. His recent exhibition at the Vancouver Art Gallery, *I Had an Interesting French Artist to See Me This Summer: Emily Carr and Wolfgang Paalen in British Columbia* (2016), explored the brief encounter between these two modernist artists in Victoria, BC, in August 1939, and presented the first extensive exhibition of Paalen's work in Canada. His collaboration with composer Alfredo Santa Ana, *Music for a Night in May*, was presented at the Vancouver East Cultural Centre in May 2018. Recent essays exploring the links between surrealism and the art of the Northwest Coast have appeared in exhibition catalogues in Canada, the United States, and Europe. He is currently working on new projects and preparing a collection of essays for publication. Until recently, he taught in the School for the Contemporary Arts at Simon Fraser University (Vancouver) where he is Professor Emeritus.